ROBINSON'S PRAYER AT THE DEPARTURE OF THE PILGRIMS FROM DELPH HAVEN.

GOULD AND LINCOLN,
BOSTON.

PLYMOUTH

AND THE

PILGRIMS;

OR

INCIDENTS OF ADVENTURE IN THE HISTORY
OF THE FIRST SETTLERS.

JOSEPH BANVARD.

BOSTON:
GOULD AND LINCOLN,
59 WASHINGTON STREET.
1851.

STEREOTYPED AT THE
BOSTON STEREOTYPE FOUNDRY.

PREFACE.

The history of our country is full of interest. The annals of our own Commonwealth, and especially of our Pilgrim fathers, abound with vivid illustrations of fearless courage, enduring fortitude, ingenious strategy, and romantic adventure.

The object of the present volume is to give a plain and correct account of the prominent events which have occurred in the history of Plymouth, the oldest colony in New England. We, of course, have not given all the incidents, neither could we in a volume of reasonable size. We have confined ourselves to the more interesting and important.

Such facts only are related as we presumed would afford entertainment and instruction to the mass of the people, and especially to the youth. A glance at the table of contents will show the nature and variety of our subjects. We have indulged in only a few moral reflections, but have furnished materials eminently suggestive of them. We present facts; our readers can deduce their own inferences.

In the preparation of the work we have availed ourselves of the most reliable sources of information from the journals and letters of the first Pilgrims down to historians of a recent date.

Each of the engravings is illustrative of some incident of which we have given an account.

NOTICE.

THE Publishers, in presenting to the reading public this first volume of Rev. Mr. Banvard's Series of American Histories, are happy to announce that other volumes of the series are in course of preparation.

This series of Histories will be made up of interesting and important events which have occurred in the United States since the first settlement of the country; illustrating, the trials and adventures of the early colonists both at the North and the South, their intercourse and conflicts with the natives, their peculiarities of character and manners, the gradual development of their institutions, sketches of their prominent men in both the Church and the State, incidents in the Revolution, with various other subjects of interest of more recent date. It is intended to be adapted to the popular mind, and especially to the youth of our country, illustrated with numerous fine engravings. There will be twelve or more 18mo. volumes, consisting of about three hundred pages each; each volume to be complete in itself; and yet, when all are published, they will, together, form a regular SERIES OF CONSECUTIVE AMERICAN HISTORY.

LIST

OF

ILLUSTRATIONS.

I. ROBINSON'S PRAYER AT THE DEPARTURE OF THE PILGRIMS FROM DELPH HAVEN.

II. ILLUSTRATED TITLE PAGE.

III. MAP OF MASSACHUSETTS BAY 18

IV. THE COPPER CHAIN 60

V. FIVE KERNELS OF CORN 140

VI. SIR CHRISTOPHER GARDNER TAKEN 169

VII. CAPTURE OF ANNAWON BY STRATAGEM..... 252

VIII. LIKENESS OF MISS REBECCA RAWSON........ 198

IX. PRISONERS IN STOCKS 206

CONTENTS.

CHAPTER I.

PAGE

A Vessel. — Something unusual on Board. — Sympathy. — Pastor's Prayer. — Separation. — Arrival at Southampton. — Robinson's Letter. — Division of the Company. — Choice of Officers. — Departure from England. — Put back to Dartmouth. — Start again. — Return to Plymouth. — One Vessel abandoned. — The other starts alone. — Storms. — Death at Sea. — Disheartening Event. —" Land." — Cape Cod Harbor. — Puritan Pilgrims. — Thanks. — The Compact. — Election of Governor. — The Men ashore. — Their Discoveries. — The Shallop. — An Expedition proposed........................... 19

CHAPTER II.

Exploring Party. — See Indians. — Their Pursuit and Behavior. — Night. — Pursuit renewed. — Great Thirst. — The first Drink of New England Water. — Deer. — Indian Graves. — Corn found buried. — Large Kettle. —A Fort.—River discovered.—Encampment in a stormy Night. — The Party lost. — Trap found in the Woods. — Reasons for minute Description. — Strength of Principle. —Water Excursion. — A Party land. — Mummies discovered. — Wigwams and Contents. — First Birth. — Third Excursion. — Midnight Alarm. — Skirmish with the Indians. — Thanks for Victory. —

Storm and Danger. — Clark's Island. — Sabbath observed. — Landing of the Pilgrims. — Division of the Land. — Commence building. — Fire. — Two Men lost. — Their Adventures. — The first Sabbath on the main Land. — The first Winter. — The Number of Immigrants. — Suffering. — Deaths. — Place called Plymouth. — Return of the Mayflower.. 29

CHAPTER III.

A strange Visitor. — Unexpected Salutation. — Information given. — A Difficulty. — Kidnapper. — Indians enslaved. — More Visitors. — Squanto's Adventures. — Indian Chiefs. — Visit of Ceremony. — First Treaty. — The Visit returned. — Massasoit's Poverty. — Novel Mode of Eeling. — First Offence. — The Penalty. — Billington's Character. — First Duel. — Peculiar Punishment. — Praying for Mercy. — Character of the Government.......................... 42

CHAPTER IV.

Plymouth in Summer. — Annoyance of Indian Loungers. — Visit to Massasoit. — Delivery of Presents. — The Message. — The Copper Chain. — Hard Lodging. — Subordinate Sachems. — Sports. — Shooting Fish. — Return of the Messengers. — Storm at Night. — Effect of the Visit. — Boy missing. — A Party sent after him. — Their Adventures. — Get News of the Boy. — Iyanough. — An old Squaw. — Her violent Passion. — Reason of it. — How she is pacified. — Indian Officiousness. — The Owner of the buried Corn found. — The lost Boy restored. — Natives rewarded. — Rumors of War. — Danger of the Colony.. 51

CHAPTER V.

Startling Rumors. — Squanto reconnoitres. — Is taken. — Designs against him. — Supposed Murder. — Party sent to Middleborough. — Midnight Attack. — Frightened Indians. — Squanto found. —

Treatment of the Wounded. — Voyage to Massachusetts. — Origin of the Name. — Conduct of the Squaws. — The first Summer in Plymouth. — Preparations for Winter. — Colony alarmed. — Prepare to resist Invaders. — Pleasant Disappointment. — Arrival of the Fortune. — She brings no Stores. — The Consequence. — The Fortune returns. — Her Cargo and Capture.......... 61

CHAPTER VI.

Singular Visitor. — Mysterious Package for Squanto. — The Visitor made a Captive. — His Disclosures. — He is released and sent home with a bold Message. — Squanto explains the Package. — A Package of Powder and Balls sent in Reply to it. — It is regarded with Terror. — Finally sent back unopened. — Defensive Preparations. — First General Muster. — An Indian's Advice. — Another Expedition. — Signal for Return. — Why called back. — Hobbamock denies Indian Rumors. — Squanto falls under Suspicion. — His deceitful Conduct. — Buried Plague. — Massasoit demands Squanto's Death. — The Messengers ready to kill him. — His unexpected Deliverance. — Messengers offended. — More Immigrants. — Winslow sent to Maine for Food. — Massacre in Virginia. — Fort built. — Used as a Church. — Puritan Character.......... 69

CHAPTER VII.

Arrival of the Charity and the Swan. — A New Colony. — Its Materials. — Its Object. — Its Difficulties. — An Expedition in Partnership. — Chatham. — Shyness of the Natives. — Success in Trade. — Squanto dies. — His last Request. — His History. — Favorable Providence. — Indiscretion of the New Colony. — Storm. — The Shallop aground. — Stores left in the Care of Indians. — The Return. — Puritan Firmness. — Indian Theft. — Restoration demanded. — Its Result. — Ludicrous Ceremony. — Folly of Imitation. — Indian Gamblers. — Mysterious Visitors. — Their Object. — Indian Brawl and Murder. — Hobbamock's Advice. — A Powwow executed..... 81

CHAPTER VIII.

Fears of Conspiracy. — Illness of Massasoit. — Winslow, with two others, sets out to visit him. — Arrives at a Ferry. — Hears that Massasoit is dead. — Hobbamock's deep Grief. — His Description of the Chief. — They visit Corbitant's House. — A Messenger sent to Pokanoket. — Returns with the News that Massasoit is yet alive. — The Party press on. — Their Arrival. — Powwows at work upon the sick Chief. — Winslow prescribes for him. — He improves. — Eats too hearty, and becomes worse. — Indian Custom. — Efforts to persuade Massasoit to oppose the English. — They are unsuccessful. — Massasoit reveals the Conspiracy. — His Advice. — Conversation with Corbitant. — How the Puritans taught the Indians. — Origin of Traditions...... 92

CHAPTER IX.

Condition of Weston's Colony. — Man drowned in digging Clams. — Indian Policy. — The Men rob them. — Indians complain. — A slanderous Tradition. — Butler perpetuates it. — Its Origin. — Plymouth not responsible for Weymouth. — Consultation of the two Colonies. — Sanders goes to Maine for Provisions. — Dangers of the English. — Their Perils considered by the Court. — Standish sent to Weymouth to capture Indians. — His Instructions. — Insulting Conduct of the Indians. — Pratt's providential Escape. — He relates the wretched Condition of Weymouth. — Pratt is pursued. — His Pursuer captured as a Spy. — Standish arrives at Weymouth. — Makes known the Conspiracy. — The Captain's Policy. — Indians pretend they know his Object. — Their Insults. — The boasting of Indian Braves. — The forbearance of the Captain...... 104

CHAPTER X.

Silent, but fearful Massacre. — Hobbamock compliments Standish. — Women held Captives. — An Indian escapes. — Three Englishmen among the Indians. — The Indians haste away at Midnight. —

They meet Standish and his Men. — A Skirmish. — The Indians defeated. — Hobbamock's Bravery. — The Indian Women released uninjured. — The Puritans responsible for the Massacre. — Their Apology. — A young Indian's Confession. — Standish returns, taking an Indian's Head. — The captured Spy recognizes it. — The Spy released and sent as a Messenger. — A Squaw brings back an Answer. — The three Englishmen killed. — The Terror of the Natives. — They attempt to send a Peace-offering to the Governor. — The Boat is wrecked. — Robinson's Letter........................ 118

CHAPTER XI.

The Conspiracy checked. — Arrival of a Blacksmith in disguise. — Who he is. — He hears unwelcome News. — He sails for Weymouth. — Is cast away and robbed. — Kindness of the Puritans. — Repaid with Ingratitude. — The Puritans without a Charter. — The Advantage of it. — Their first Patent. — The Ambition of John Pierce. — Is disappointed. — Arrival of more Immigrants and Stores. — The Distress of the Colony. — Admiral West. — Cannot subdue the Fishermen. — Community of Goods abandoned. — Self-Dependence. — Its Results. — The five Kernels of Corn. — No Bread. — Patience of the Sufferers. — Long Drought. — Day of Fasting and Prayer. — Refreshing Showers. — Effect upon the Natives.. 129

CHAPTER XII.

John Lyford. — His Obsequiousness. — His Connection with John Oldham. — Governor Bradford takes Copies of their Letters. — Oldham rebels. — Lyford sets up a Meeting. — Their Trial. — The Governor's Address. — Both found guilty. — Oldham banished. — Lyford's Confession and deep Sorrow. — Repeats his Offence. — Oldham returns. — His abusive Conduct. — Sentenced to run the Gantlet. — He reforms. — Is killed by the Indians. — Timely Abundance. — Trade with the Kennebec. — Return Ship captured.—

Escape of Standish from Slavery. — Death of John Robinson. — His Character. — Death of Robert Cushman. — He preached the first Sermon in New England. — Its Character. — Extracts........ 141

CHAPTER XIII.

A Pinnace built. — Messengers from the Dutch. — Reception of De Razier. — Trade with him. — Wampum. — The Colony without a Pastor. — Original Agreement respecting their old Pastor. — A Minister found at Nantasket. — He becomes the Plymouth Pastor. — His Character. — Roger Williams. — His Troubles at Salem. — Goes to Plymouth as an Assistant. — Returns to Salem. — He cultivates Acquaintance with the Natives. — John Billington. — Commits Murder. — Is tried and executed. — The Tendency of Sin. — A Shipwreck. — Kindness of the Indians. — Difficulties adjusted. — Governor Winthrop's Visit to Plymouth. — Singular Puritan Custom. — Discussion about the Use of "Goodman Such-a-one." — Hue's Cross 154

CHAPTER XIV.

Sir Christopher Gardner. — Foments Trouble. — Is charged with Bigamy. — Is pursued. — Is delivered up by Indians. — Indian Custom to secure a Welcome. — Small-pox. — Trade extended. — Adventures on the Connecticut. — Troubles on the Kennebec. — Captain Hocking killed. — A Plymouth Magistrate arrested in Boston. — Excitement at Plymouth. — Deputies sent to Boston. — Prayer before Business. — The Defence. — The Confession. — The Adjustment. — A Hurricane. — Its dreadful Ravages. — Eclipse of the Moon....... 167

CHAPTER XV.

An Indian murdered. — Four Englishmen in Want. — They visit Roger Williams. — Are found to be the Murderers. — Three are caught. — Their Trial. — Singular Difficulty. — Their Execution. —

Effect of Puritan Justice on the Indians. — Anecdote of Captain Standish. — Alden takes his new Bride home on a Bull. — Confederation of the New England Colonies. — Germ of the American Union. — Its Influence. — Indian Alliances. — The Removal of the whole Colony proposed. — Subject considered by the Church. — Purchase Eastham. — Found to be more unfavorable than Plymouth. — The Project abandoned. — Ex-Governor Prince settles at Eastham 176

CHAPTER XVI.

Quakers ordered out of the Colony. — They refuse to obey. — All forbidden to harbor Quakers. — Humphrey Norton imprisoned. — Quakers' Contempt of Government. — Insolence to the Governor. — Refuse to take Oath. — Are whipped. — Norton's Letters. — Fanaticism always troublesome. — No Quaker or Ranter permitted to be a Freeman. — A House of Correction ordered to be built. — Six Quakers banished on Pain of Death. — Milder Laws. — Four Persons appointed to reason with them. — One of these becomes a Quaker. — All Persons authorized to arrest them. — Their Meetings forbidden. — Severity excites Sympathy. — Rigorous Measures were not universally approved. — Charles II. ascends the Throne of England. — He suppresses the Persecutions. — Secretary Rawson. — His Daughter Rebecca receives the attentions of Thomas Rumsey. — Marries him. — Accompanies him to England. — Finds a Relative. — Conduct of her Husband. — Painful Discovery. — Her Abandonment. — Her Self-reliance. — Embarks for Jamaica. — Arrival there. — Her unhappy End 185

CHAPTER XVII.

The Enactment of Law develops Character. — Trial by Jury. — Wants of the Colony to be supplied first. — Exports forbidden. — Those who refused the Office of Governor to be fined. — Bradford released by Importunity. — How different now. — Marriage forbidden without the Consent of Parents. — Intentions of Marriage to be published. — Consent of Parents to be obtained to address their Daughters. — Punishment to depend upon "Quality" of the Offender. — Short Sleeves forbidden. — Laws against Contempt of the Scriptures. — Sabbath-breaking and Gambling Laws executed. — Stocks and Cage always ready. — Psalm Singing. — Courtship punished. — Abuse of Husbands. — Blackbirds' Heads to be obtained. — Effects of Union of Church and State. — Every Colony to have a Church. — Church Rates. — Whales. — Ministers forbidden to leave their People. — Meeting-house in every Town. — Parental Instruction. — Schools. — Arms must be taken to Meeting. — Indians and Wolves. — Effects of these Laws. — The Bible the Basis of their Legislation. 199

CHAPTER XVIII.

Fifty Years of Peace. — New Settlements. — Converted Indians. — Native Preachers. — Philip and the Button. — Indian Magistrates. — Indian Warrant. — Alexander succeeds Massasoit. — Suspicions against him. — His Death. — Philip becomes Grand Sachem. — Pursues John Gibbs for reviling the Dead. — His Alliance with the Narragansetts. — He desires Revenge. — Ordered to come to Plymouth. — Declines. — Invites the Governor to come to him. — They meet at Taunton. — Singular Scene in a Church. — The Treaty. — Indignant Sachem. — Treaty violated. — Conference at Plymouth. — Indian Confederacy. — Philip's deep Plot against the English. — Their Security. — Philip angry with Sassamon. — The latter flees to the English. — The Plot revealed. — Sassamon missing. — Philip again examined. — No Confession. — Suspicions increase. 212

CHAPTER XIX.

Harvard College. — Indian Students. — Sassamon. — Search for him. — Body found. — Murderers arrested and executed. — Philip enraged. — Preparations for Conflict. — Bold Language. — Opinion respecting the first Fire. — Indians pant for Plunder. — War begun. — English killed on Fast Day. — Excitement in the Colonies. —

Enlisting Recruits in Boston. — Bridgewater Horsemen. — People driven from their burning Houses. — The English surprised and slain. — Affecting Scene. — Philip pursued. — Found at Dinner. — Escapes. — Mutilated Englishmen. — Fuller's narrow Escape. — Church's brave Adventure. — Golding's timely Arrival. — Marvellous Preservation. — Church's Visit to the Spring amidst a Shower of Balls 224

CHAPTER XX.

Philip retreats to a Swamp. — An Ambush. — Wigwams found. — Philip escapes by Water. — Route discovered. — Ministers fight. — Philip overtaken. — A Battle ensues. — The War becomes general. — Its Consequences. — Disgraceful Conduct towards the Dartmouth Indians. — Sold into Slavery. — Influence on other Tribes. — Philip's Ravages in Plymouth. — Retreats to a Swamp. — The Swamp surrounded. — Philip shot. — The Enemy routed. — The Gun preserved. — Philip beheaded and quartered. — His Head and Hand preserved. — Bitter Spirit of the English. — His Head exposed many Years 236

CHAPTER XXI.

The War not ended. — Annawon holds out. — Prowls around the Town. — Church goes in Pursuit. — Captures a Party of Indians. — Man seeking his Father. — Church discovers a Path. — Takes an old Indian and young Girl. — Examines them. — Learns Annawon's Retreat. — Old Man becomes Guide. — He refuses to fight against his Chief. — Leads them to Annawon's Encampment. — High Rock. — Exciting Scene. — Church's Stratagem. — Its Execution. — Annawon surprised. — The whole Band captured. — Leaders cannot sleep. — Philip's Ornaments delivered up. — Church's Anxiety. — Morning. — Prisoners taken to Plymouth. — What shall be done with them? — Opinion of Ministers. — Young Annawon. — Prisoners sold into Slavery. — Church opposed to it 245

CHAPTER XXII.

The Colonies affected by the Home Government. — Arrival of Andros. — Encourages Episcopacy. — Declares Land Titles invalid. — Appropriates public Property to private Uses. — Prohibits Town Meetings. — Other Oppressions. — Andros imprisoned. — Nathaniel Clark seized. — Clark's Island. — The first Sabbath. — Wiswall imprisoned. — Absence from Town Meetings fined. — A Price for Wolves' Heads. — The first Selectmen. — The first Marriage. — An honored Lady. — Introduction of Neat Cattle. — First Record of Horses. — A Present to Philip. — Merry Mount. — Weetamore beheaded. — Its Effect on the Indians. — French Vessel wrecked. — The Crew seized as Prisoners. — Doctor Le Baron. — His Settlement and Marriage. — His Attachment to the Cross. — A Premium for Rats' Heads. — First public Celebration of "The Landing." — The Dinner. — The famous Rock. — Its Locality proved. — The Evidence of Elder Faunce and others. — The Rock splits. — A good Omen. — Is removed. — Treatment of Tories. — Wonderful Egg. — Dreadful Shipwreck. — Statistics........................ 257

CHAPTER XXIII.

Attachment to the Scriptures. — Reason of Puritanic Singularities. — Precise in their Manners. — Their Ministers of equal Authority. — Their Government republican. — Their Self-reliance and divine Dependence. — Were not vindictive. — Did not come here to establish universal Toleration. — Their Object was Liberty for themselves. — This the Origin of their Opposition to other Sects. — The Prospective Influence of their Principles................................ 281

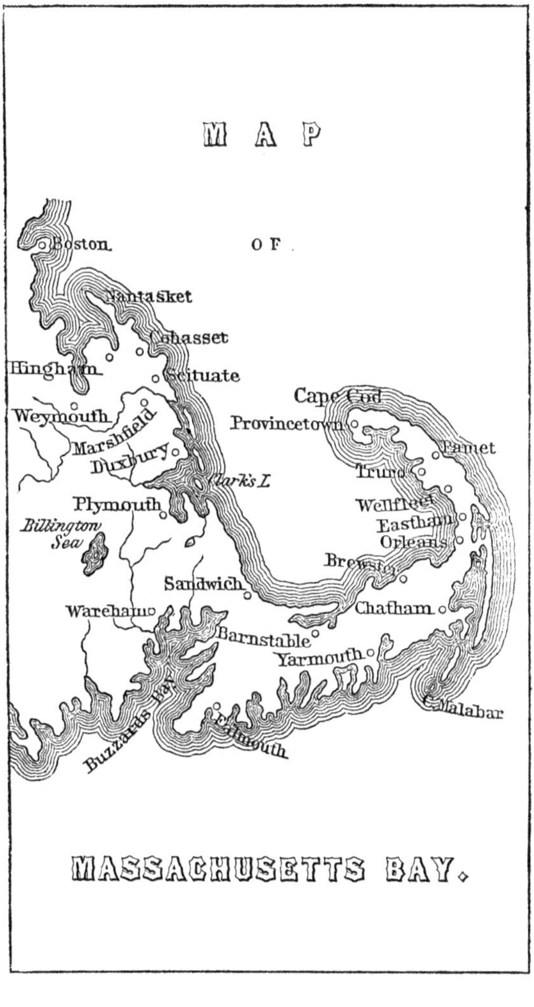

MAP

OF

Boston.
Nantasket
Cohasset
Hingham
Scituate
Weymouth
Marshfield
Duxbury
Clark's I.
Plymouth
Billington Sea
Cape Cod
Provincetown
Pamet
Truro
Wellfleet
Eastham
Orleans
Brewster
Sandwich
Wareham
Chatham
Barnstable
Yarmouth
Buzzards Bay
Falmouth
C. Malabar

MASSACHUSETTS BAY.

CHAPTER I.

> "They crowd the strand,
> Those few, lone pilgrims. Can ye scan the woe
> That wrings their bosoms, as the last frail link
> Binding to man and habitable earth
> Is severed? Can ye tell what pangs were there,
> What keen regrets, what sickness of the heart,
> What yearning o'er their forfeit land of birth;
> Their distant, dear ones?" — SIGOURNEY.

A Vessel. — Something unusual on Board. — Sympathy. — Pastor's Prayer. — Separation. — Arrival at Southampton. — Robinson's Letter. — Division of the Company. — Choice of Officers. — Departure from England. — Put back to Dartmouth. — Start again. — Return to Plymouth. — One Vessel abandoned. — The other starts alone. — Storms. — Death at Sea. — Disheartening Event. — "Land." — Cape Cod Harbor. — Puritan Pilgrims. — Thanks. — The Compact. — Election of Governor. — The Men ashore. — Their Discoveries. — The Shallop. — An Expedition proposed.

ABOUT July 22, in the year of our Lord 1620, at Delph Haven, in Holland, might have been seen a company of devout Christian men and women on board of a frail vessel of peculiar structure. A casual observer might have perceived that something unusual was in progress. Little groups were standing here and there in earnest conversation; others, by themselves, were looking over the sides of the vessel, or gazing with deep interest upon objects with which they were familiar, but which they never expected to behold again. Some were hurrying to and fro, making rapid inquiries, to ascertain that nothing which they needed on board was left behind. Friends who sympathized with them had come from a distance to give them the parting hand, and pronounce upon them their farewell blessing. When the hour of their departure arrived, and they could tarry no longer among those whom they loved so well, their pastor, Rev. John Robinson, falling upon his knees in the midst of the little company, who also knelt around him, commended them, in a most fervent prayer, to the kind protection of their heavenly Father. After the religious services were over, "with mutual embraces," they took their leave of those who were to remain behind.

"Truly doleful was the sight," says Governor Bradford, "of that sad and mournful parting; to see what sighs and sobs and prayers did sound amongst them; what tears did gush from every eye, and pithy speeches pierced each other's heart, that sundry of the Dutch strangers that stood on the quay as spectators could not refrain from tears." Winslow, who was with the company on board, says, that when they separated, "We gave them a volley of small shot, and three pieces of ordnance, and so lifting up our hands to each other, and our hearts for each other to the Lord our God, we departed, and found his presence with us." They directed their course to Southampton, where they found a larger vessel, commanded by Captain Jones, waiting for them, as were also Mr. Cushman and the rest of the church, who were to accompany them across the pathless waters to a new world.

Whilst they were tarrying there, they received a letter from their pastor, at Leyden, Rev. John Robinson, who, though he could not accompany them, cherished a deep interest in the success of their enterprise, and who availed himself of this early opportunity to send them an epistle filled with judicious counsels and cautions. The company were soon called together, and listened with great pleasure to the valuable advice of their religious guide. They were then divided into two parties for the two ships. In order that every thing might be properly conducted on board of their respective vessels, each party, with the permission of their captain, chose a governor and two or three assistants, who were to exercise over them a general supervision.

On the 5th of August, the two vessels, the names of which were the Mayflower and the Speedwell, left Southampton on their perilous voyage. But they had not sailed far, before the Speedwell, which was the smaller vessel of the two, was found to be in a very leaky condition. It was deemed dangerous to proceed. This was peculiarly unfortunate

They both put back to Dartmouth, where the vesse was examined and repaired. She was found to be in such bad condition, that if she had continued at sea but a few hours longer, she must have sunk.

About the 21st of August, they ventured to sea once more, and after having advanced above a hundred leagues, the same vessel was found to leak again, more badly, if possible, than before. They returned now to Plymouth. Upon a second examination, as no important leak was found, the trouble was attributed to her general weakness, on which account she was reluctantly abandoned as an unsafe craft in which to encounter the dangers of the Atlantic. But it was afterwards ascertained that the whole difficulty was caused by the deceitfulness of the captain and crew of the Speedwell. They had engaged to remain in the new country, whither they were going, a whole year; but they repented of their bargain. They feared that when the provisions which they carried with them were exhausted, they would be unable to obtain more, and consequently would perish from famine. They therefore pretended that their vessel was not sea-worthy, in order to have an excuse for retreating from their engagement, and tarrying behind. Some of them afterwards confessed their timidity, and revealed the stratagem. After the abandonment of the Speedwell, as it was found impossible to accommodate all of her passengers in the other ship, some of them were compelled to relinquish the voyage. This gave occasion for another painful separation. Among those who remained behind was Mr. Robert Cushman, who had been deeply interested in the arrangements and objects of the emigration, and who afterwards took a prominent part in the history of the colony.

Captain Jones, of the Mayflower, received on board his vessel as many of the passengers of the Speedwell as, with their stores, it was safe for him to carry, and on the 6th of September, started alone. The little vessel, freighted with the future liberties and glory of a great nation, was soon overtaken by violent storms, which strained her, rendered her leaky, and cracked one of the "main beams of the mid-ships." Fears were entertained that she would never reach her destined shores. One of the passengers having brought "a great iron screw from Holland," it was employed in bringing the broken beam into its place again, where it was securely fastened by the carpenter. The storm continued to rage so furiously that not a single sail could be used, and they were tossed helplessly about for many days together, like a feather upon the boisterous waves. An additional ingredient in their cup of sorrow was the unwelcome visit of death. To one of their number the green bed of the ocean furnished a grave. A burial at sea is always impressive. The solemnity of the ship's company; the placing of the corpse on the narrow plank; the brief prayer — perhaps the absence of prayer; the raising of the corpse to the side of the vessel by those who had been the cheerful companions of the deceased thus far; the last look; the launch into the sea; the sullen, gurgling plunge; its disappearance without leaving a trace behind; and the sense of loss which the survivors feel; — all combined, serve to render such a catastrophe deeply affecting; but, in the present instance, it was unusually so. This band of pilgrims were on their way to a country destitute of civilized inhabitants. They were about to form a settlement in an inhospitable clime, and among savage men, three thousand miles from their own land. Their whole number would be sufficiently small to be placed in such perilous circumstances, so far from those who could aid them, in case help should be needed. To all appearance they could spare none. When, therefore, this death occurred on their voyage, it must have been a disheartening event. It must have served to deepen their sense of dependence upon that great and good Being, under whose auspices the enterprise was commenced, and without whose constant care it would inevitably fail.

November 9, the cheering cry was heard, "Land, land!" It proved to be Cape Cod. As it was their design to commence their settlements in the vicinity of Hudson's River, they steered their course southerly to reach the mouth of that noble stream. They soon found themselves among shoals and breakers. As the wind subsided, they discovered that they were in danger and could not proceed. They retraced their course, and by the next day arrived at the Cape Harbor.

This band of adventurers were PURITAN PILGRIMS, who, because they could not enjoy liberty of conscience in their own country, had most unwillingly, and at great sacrifice, left it, in order that they might find a place where they could worship God, and enjoy the ordinances of religion according to their own views of duty, without the opposition of the civil power. Another object which they had in view, and which they ever kept constantly before them, was the conversion of the natives of the country whither they were going — the savage and superstitious Indians, to Christianity.

As every thing connected with the landing and the first settlement of these Pilgrims is both interesting and instructive, we shall enter somewhat into the details of their early adventures.

The Puritans were men of prayer. In all undertakings of importance, they were accustomed to seek direction from their heavenly Father, and implore his blessing. Accordingly, on Saturday,

3

November 11, religious services were held on board of the Mayflower. They fell on their knees, rendered thanks to God for his kind protection of them during their dangerous voyage across the ocean, and implored his favor to rest upon them amid the toils, trials, and temptations upon which they were now to enter.

As some of the party were "not well affected to unity and concord, but gave some appearance of faction," it was deemed advisable to enter into a mutual compact or agreement. Accordingly, a document was prepared, in which they said, "Having undertaken, for the glory of God and the advancement of the Christian faith and honor of our king and country, a voyage to plant the first colony in the northern parts of Virginia, we do, by these presents, solemnly and mutually, in the presence of God and one another, covenant and combine ourselves together into a civil body politic, for our better ordering, and preservation, and furtherance of the ends aforesaid; and by virtue hereof to enact, constitute, and frame such just and equal laws, ordinances, acts, constitutions, and offices, from time to time, as shall be thought most meet and convenient for the general good of the colony; unto which we promise all due submission and obedience."

This important document, which was "the birth

of popular constitutional liberty," was signed by all the men. It was the formation of a government of "equal laws" for "the general good." It was the germ of those free institutions which are now diffusing liberty, prosperity, and happiness throughout our highly-favored New England. Its influence upon the subsequent history of our country cannot be too highly valued.

Their next measure was the election of a governor for the year. Their choice fell upon John Carver, who is described as "a pious and well-approved gentleman." The high estimation in which he was held is evinced by the fact that he was chosen unanimously. Thus their government was formed and their governor chosen before they left the deck of the Mayflower!

The same day, a company of fifteen or sixteen men, well armed, so as to defend themselves against the Indians, went on shore to obtain wood, as their stock on board was exhausted, and also to examine the land, and discover, if possible, inhabitants. They found the country covered with trees of various kinds, among which were sassafras, juniper, walnut, ash, birch, oaks, and pines. These were free from under-bush, so that they might have rode among them without inconvenience. No inhabitants were seen. They loaded their boat with juniper, to which they were partial for fuel, as, in burning, it exhaled a pleasant fragrance. They returned the same night. The cold season was rapidly advancing. Some of the company had been cooped up in the narrow limits of the Mayflower over a hundred days. A place for their disembarkation and settlement was yet to be selected. They naturally felt solicitous to get their shallop out, and make explorations along the shore in search of good winter quarters. As they had been obliged to cut it down in order to stow it between decks, and as the people had used it for a sleeping berth on the voyage, it was found to be in great need of repairs. Sixteen or seventeen tedious days was the carpenter employed in making it sea-worthy. As no Indians were at hand to molest them, the men went on shore for amusement, and the women to wash. Some of the men desired to make excursions into the country, for purposes of discovery. Others thought that it would be a dangerous experiment. However, a party of sixteen men was placed under the command of Captain Miles Standish, with whom were appointed, as counsellors and advisers, William Bradford, Stephen Hopkins, and Edward Tilley. After receiving many cautions and directions how to proceed in case of peculiar emergencies, they departed. The adventures with which they met will be narrated in the next chapter.

CHAPTER II.

" By yon wave-beaten rock,
See the illustrious flock
Collected stand;
To seek some sheltering grove,
Their faithful partners move,
Dear pledges of their love
In either hand. — JOHN DAVIS.

Exploring Party. — See some Indians. — Their Pursuit and Behavior. — Night. — Pursuit renewed. — Great Thirst. — The first Drink of New England Water. — Deer. — Indian Graves. — Corn found buried. — Large Kettle. — A Fort. — River discovered. — Encampment in a stormy Night. — The Party lost. — A Trap found in the Woods. — Reasons for minute Description. — Strength of Principle. — Water Excursion. — A Party land. — Mummies discovered. — Wigwams and Contents. — First Birth. — Third Excursion. — Midnight Alarm. — Skirmish with the Indians. — Thanks for Victory. — Storm and Danger. — Clark's Island. — Sabbath observed. — Landing of the Pilgrims. — Division of the Land. — Commence building. — Fire. — Two Men Lost. — Their Adventures. — The first Sabbath on the main Land. — The first Winter. — The Number of Immigrants. — Suffering. — Deaths. — Place called Plymouth. — Return of the Mayflower.

THE party of sixteen, after they had received their instructions, went on shore. They arranged themselves in single file, and after marching in this manner about a mile, they saw five or six individuals advancing towards them, accompanied by a dog. They were Indians, the first they had seen since their arrival. When the savages discovered the party, they immediately fled. The men followed them by their trail for ten miles. Night coming on, their pursuit was stopped. They gathered wood, kindled a fire, set three for sentinels, and encamped till morning. As soon as it was sufficiently light for them to discover the tracks of the Indians, they renewed their pursuit. Their course was greatly impeded by the woods and bushes through which they passed, and which tore their "very armor in pieces." They were unsuccessful in overtaking them; neither did they discover any villages or single tents. As they took with them no water, and had discovered none which they could drink since they left the ship, they suffered much from thirst. They had with them a "little bottle of *aquavitæ*," but that was far from affording them the needed relief. However, they persevered in their journey, and about the middle of the forenoon they entered a deep valley, in which were many little paths running in different directions. To their great joy, they here found several springs of fresh water, from which they obtained an abundant supply. "We were heartily glad," say they in their journal, "and sat us down and drunk our first New England water with as much delight as ever we drunk drink in all our lives." They here discovered some deer. The narrow tracks which they saw were probably made by deer and other animals when going to the springs to drink. Leaving this refreshing valley, they directed their course to the south. When they reached the shore, they kindled a fire to indicate their position to those on board the ship. Passing on farther, they came to several small sand-hills covered with mats, with a wooden object shaped something like a mortar on the top, with an earthern pot placed in a small hole at the end. They dug into them, and found a bow and some decayed arrows. Supposing them to be Indian sepulchres, they replaced these objects, and restored the hills to their original appearance. They were unwilling to irritate the natives by plundering the graves of their friends. They passed by some pieces of land where stubble was standing, from which the corn had been recently gathered, and where a house had formerly stood. They found a large kettle which had probably belonged to some ship, and also a great quantity of corn, red, yellow, and blue, some shelled and some in the ear. A part of the corn was contained in a round basket, narrow at the top, and a part was buried in the ground. They filled the kettle with corn for two men to carry between them. They also stowed as much in their pockets as they conveniently could. The remainder they buried again. Their intention was, if they could obtain an interview with any of the natives, to pay them for the corn, and return them the kettle if they wanted it.

Not far from this place they came to a rude fort. They next discovered a river, in which they saw two canoes. They were now obliged to return, as they had orders to be absent only two days. They retraced their steps to the spring of fresh water. Here they erected a rough barricade to keep of the wind, built a fire, appointed their sentinels, and passed the night as comfortably as they could in a heavy storm of rain. In the morning they sunk the kettle in a pond, "trimmed" their muskets anew, as they could not be fired in consequence of the wet, and pressed towards the ship. On their return, they lost their way, and were at their "wits' end" to know what course to pursue. Whilst they were wandering about, they came to a trap made by bending down the small branch of a tree, with a rope-noose attached. It had probably been set by the Indians to take deer. As they were examining it, it suddenly sprang, and caught one of the party by the leg. It exhibited considerable ingenuity. They also saw great numbers of wild geese and ducks, a few partridges, and three bucks. At last they came in sight of the ship. They fired off their guns as a signal, when those on board immediately sent the long-boat, and gave them a hearty welcome home. With what interest did their friends gather around them to hear the story of their adventures! How many questions they asked respecting those Indians, the springs, the graves, the kettle, the canoes, the trap! With what joy did they examine the corn of divers colors! They must have regarded it somewhat as the Jews did the grapes of Eschol, which were brought back by the spies who were sent to examine the land. It was the first fruits of the land of promise. Soon, snow began to fall.

We have been thus particular in giving these details, because this was the first excursion of the Puritan Pilgrims in New England, where they had come to seek a home for themselves, their wives, and their children. What strength of religious principle, what moral and physical courage, what self-denial, and what strong confidence in God must have been requisite to induce them to disembark and commence the settlement of this comparatively barren country, with nothing over them but the heavens enshrouded with clouds, and the earth around them covered with snow, as if Nature were enrobed in the winding-sheet of death. The incidents of their early history should never be forgotten.

Their next excursion was on the water, in their frail shallop. The number of this party was thirty-four, ten of whom were sailors who belonged to the ship. They had a severe time, very different from the pleasure excursions which are now made in the same waters every year. The wind blew strong, the waves ran high, the snow fell, and the spray, as it dashed upon them, was converted to ice. Some of them became so chilled, and took such severe colds as afterwards resulted in death. A portion of them landed, but soon became "tired with marching up and down the steep hills and deep valleys which lay half a foot thick with snow." They encamped for the night under a few pine-trees. As they had eaten nothing since the morning, three fat geese and six ducks which they obtained furnished them with a very acceptable supper.

When they arrived at Pamet River where the previous party had seen the two canoes, they ferried themselves across.

They next visited the place where the corn and kettle were obtained. They found a bottle of oil, a bag of beans, some wheat ears, and seven or eight bushels more of corn. They came upon a grave much larger than any they had seen before. It was covered with boards. After some hesitation they opened it, not knowing, from its external appearance, what it was. It contained mats, broaches, bowls, dishes, trinkets, and two large bundles. These bundles were very peculiar. The larger one contained the bones and skull of a human being, enveloped in a great quantity of fine red powder, with a knife, a large needle, and several implements of iron, whose use they could not determine. In the smaller one was the skeleton of a child. It was accompanied with strings, bracelets of fine white beads, a small bow, and "some other odd knackes." The red powder yielded a strong, though not unpleasant odor, and seemed to have been used for the purpose of embalming. They selected some of the most interesting articles to take away with them, and, covering up the rest, they left the grave, in appearance, as they found it.

They came across a couple of Indian tents, destitute of inhabitants, but containing a variety of baskets, bowls, pots, trays, dishes, with eagles' claws, deer's heads and hoofs, harts' horns, and other articles in use among the Indians. After rambling about in various directions, without any important results, they returned to the vessel.

Whilst this party were absent on their explorations, a child was born on board of the Mayflower, who was named Peregrine White. This was the first English child born in New England. There are people now living, who, in their early years, were acquainted with persons who had seen and conversed with Peregrine. He was then removed from such survivors by only one generation. This fact makes his history *seem* quite recent. He died in Marshfield, at the age of eighty-three years and eight months.

To return to the immigrants. As no place had as yet been discovered where they were willing to commence their settlement, on the sixth of December a third party went forth to make further discoveries. As they were sailing along the shore in the shallop, they saw on land about a dozen Indians, very busy in carrying something away. They afterwards discovered that it was a dead grampus, from which fact they named the place Grampus Bay, now known as Eastham. The party landed and went in pursuit of the Indians. They passed by some abandoned tents or huts, a large burying ground, and some corn-fields. Being unsuccessful in overtaking the natives, they returned to the shore and encamped. About midnight, they were disturbed by a "great and hideous cry." "Arm! arm!" shouted the sentinel. The men sprang to their feet, seized their guns, and two of them fired; but as nothing more was heard, they concluded that it must have been wolves or foxes. The next morning, after prayers were over, whilst they were preparing for another journey, they were suddenly attacked by a party of Indians, who came upon them with a great noise. A combat ensued. Unfortunately, the men were divided. Some were on the shore, and some on board the shallop. However, the guns of the Puritans were more than a match for the arrows of the Indians. The savages fled, and were followed a considerable distance. The men paused, shouted after them twice, and fired off a couple of guns to indicate to the enemy that they were not alarmed. It was supposed that they numbered thirty or forty. Their arrows, headed with eagles' claws, horn, and pieces of brass, were picked up, and afterwards sent to England. The place where this conflict occurred, they named "The First Encounter." After offering thanks to their heavenly Father for their victory, they returned to their shallop, and continued their excursion. A heavy storm of wind, rain, and snow beat upon them. Their rudder broke and became unmanageable. Presently their mast was split into three pieces. In this condition, they came very near being totally wrecked. Finally, after great anxiety and toil, they reached an island near the entrance of Plymouth harbor, where they spent the night in safety, though very uncomfortably, under the peltings of a pitiless winter storm. This was subsequently called Clark's Island, in honor of the mate of the Mayflower, who is said to have been the first who stepped upon it.

The next day being the Sabbath, they rested. We should suppose that if there is any virtue in the plea of "necessity and mercy" for attending to secular affairs on the Sabbath, it ought to have availed with them. They were houseless, friendless, and on an unknown shore, in the depth of winter, with its severities daily increasing upon them.

Their provisions were diminishing, some of their number were sick, and every hour increased the importance of their coming to a decision where to land. Yet with this combination of pressing emergencies, they refused to spend the Sabbath in seeking a harbor. Their trust was in God. They felt secure of his protection so long as they were faithful to his commandments.

The next day being Monday, December 11, old style, but the 22d, new style, they examined the harbor, and found it convenient for shipping. They then went on the main land, where Plymouth now stands, and, finding some of it cleared and some of it wooded, with plenty of springs and running brooks, they deemed it a suitable place to commence their settlement, and this was "The Landing of the Pilgrim Fathers," an event which is now annually commemorated by the descendants of the Puritans in various parts of our land, and which, in its influence upon posterity, has been followed by the most glorious results ever achieved by man.

In making arrangements for the division of the land, the whole company were divided into families, each single man joining some family. This rendered a smaller number of houses necessary. To each person they assigned a lot, half a pole in length and three in breadth, or 8¼ feet by 49½. In the erection of their houses, they incurred many difficulties. Trees had to be felled, timber hewn, holes dug in the frozen soil, and much of this they were obliged to do in the midst of very wet, cold, and stormy weather. To increase their difficulties, the Mayflower was anchored a mile and a half from the shore. As there was frequent occasion for passing to and fro, this distance subjected them to great inconvenience. Besides, as every man was intent upon finishing his own house, they could render but little assistance to each other. One building, twenty feet square, was erected as a place of common rendezvous; but this was soon accidentally burnt down, and though the house contained powder and loaded guns, and Governor Carver and William Bradford were there confined to their bed, yet no person was injured.

Two of their number being sent out to cut thatch one morning, got lost. Not returning, several others went in search of them, but without success. Sorrow filled the hearts of the company. They feared that their friends had been captured by the Indians: but the next day they returned, to the great joy of all. They lost themselves by chasing a deer. The night was wet and stormy, yet they had to spend it in the open air with wild beasts, which they supposed were lions, roaring around them. One of them, John Goodman, was frost-bitten so badly that his shoes had to be cut from his feet, and for a long time he was unable to walk. The 21st of January was the Sabbath. As the largest portion of the people were on land, they kept the Sabbath there. This appears to have been the first Lord's day which was observed upon the shore.

Indians were seen upon the water, but could not be spoken with. A house which had been built for the sick took fire from a spark, but was not much injured. Indians skulked around them, and stole the tools which the men left in the woods. All attempts to have an interview with them proved unavailing. Occasionally a few wild fowl were shot, which furnished them with a dainty repast. As a protection against the natives, who, judging from their conduct, were viciously inclined, they planted two cannon upon a hill which was near. Thus they wore away their first dreary winter upon the wild and bleak coast of New England, without any incident transpiring of special importance.

It is evident from the journals of that season that the winter was unusually mild If it had been as severe as many which have since been experienced, we see not how they could have survived till spring.

The number who left Plymouth in the Mayflower was just one hundred. One died on the passage, and one was born; so that the number who landed was one hundred. Scarcity of food, with exposure to cold' and wet, introduced disease, and, by the opening of spring, one half their number were swept away by death! To increase their affliction, among the deceased was John Carver, their governor. Some of the time two and three would die in a day. The well were not sufficient to provide for the sick, and the living hardly able to bury the dead.

The name of Plymouth was given to the new colony, as a token of respect to the inhabitants of Plymouth, in England, where the Puritans were treated with kindness when they put back in distress. After the death of Carver, William Bradford was chosen governor. The same day that Carver died, which was the 5th of April, 1621, the Mayflower sailed for England. She came to anchor in Cape Cod Harbor, November 10. She had remained, therefore, with the Pilgrims nearly five months, furnishing them with a shelter until they could get their own rough huts erected. This was a great convenience, especially to the females, the children, and the sick.

CHAPTER III.

> "Our fathers' God! thy own decree
> Ordained the Pilgrims to be free;
> In foreign lands they owned thy care,
> And found a safe asylum there." — Rev. Dr. Holmes.

A strange Visitor. — Unexpected Salutation. — Information given. — A Difficulty. — A Kidnapper. — Indians enslaved. — More Visitors. — Squanto's Adventures. — Indian Chiefs. — Visit of Ceremony. — First Treaty. — The Visit returned. — Massasoit's Poverty. — Novel Mode of Eeling. — First Offence. — The Penalty. — Billington's Character. — First Duel. — Peculiar Punishment. — Praying for Mercy. — Character of the Government.

On the morning of Friday, the 16th of March, the immigrants were alarmed by seeing an Indian enter their little village, and, with great boldness, march directly towards their place of rendezvous. Here they intercepted him, as otherwise he would have entered; when, to their surprise and joy, he accosted them in broken English, and bade them "Welcome." He was entirely naked, with the exception of a strip of leather around his waist having a fringe three or four inches long. He was tall and straight, and had long straight black hair, but no beard. His weapons were a bow and two arrows, only one of which was headed. The Pilgrims treated him with great hospitality. This was demanded both by duty and sound policy. From conversation with him, they ascertained that he was a chief of a tribe of Indians whose land was distant five days' journey. He had learned a little English from the fishermen who frequented the coast of Maine. He asked them for beer, but they gave him "strong water," biscuit, butter, cheese, pudding, and a piece of mallard. These he relished. He had acquired a taste for them by his previous intercourse with the English. He informed them that the place where they were was called Patuxet, and that about four years previously, by some dreadful pestilence, all the Indians who resided there were swept away. None now remained to claim the soil. They also obtained information from him respecting different parts of the country, what tribes inhabited them, their numbers, and the chiefs or sagamores who ruled them. Notwithstanding he was so communicative, when night came they were desirous that he should leave. This he was unwilling to do. It became then a grave question how they should dispose of him until morning. Although they were willing to listen to his conversation whilst they were awake, and had their weapons at hand, they had no inclination to sleep in his company. It was proposed that he should lodge on board the Mayflower. To this he assented; but when they attempted to go to her in the shallop, the wind was so powerful, and the water so low, that they found it impossible to succeed. They were obliged, therefore, to lodge him in one of their houses ; but as a precautionary arrangement, they kept over him a strict watch. The next day he returned to Massasoit, the chief of a tribe of Indians whom he represented as being the nearest of any to the Plymouth settlement. Another tribe, called the Nausets, were, according to his account, greatly incensed against the English. They had sufficient cause. Some years before their arrival, a shipmaster by the name of Hunt, whose name is held in merited disgrace, invited some of them on board his vessel, professedly for purposes of traffic. After some twenty or thirty had accepted his invitation, he hoisted sail and bore away to the coasts of Spain, where he sold these free sons of the forest into humiliating, disgraceful, and painful slavery. Such an atrocious crime as this they could neither forget nor forgive. They burned for revenge. It was this tribe who attacked the exploring party and were defeated, the account of which we have already given.

The savage whose unexpected visit to the Pilgrims we have now narrated, was named Samoset. When he left Plymouth, he carried with him presents of a knife, bracelet, and a ring, which were given him by the English. He promised to return within a day or two, and bring with him some of Massasoit's Indians, to open a trade in furs with the colony. He fulfilled his promise the next day. Five others came with him, dressed in their peculiar costume of deer skins, leathern leggins, and tawdry ornaments. They were hospitably received by the colonists ; but as it was the Sabbath, no business was transacted with them. They were dismissed as early as possible. Samoset, who probably fared better among the English than when with the Indians, was sick, or pretended to be, and would not return with the others. He remained till the next Wednesday. As the others did not repeat their visit, according to promise, Samoset was sent to ascertain the reason. When he left, the people gave him a hat, stockings, shoes, shirt, and a piece of cloth to wear round his body. The same day, three Indians were discovered upon a hill near by, who appeared to threaten or bid defiance to the English. Immediately, Captain Standish and three others went towards them. After making a few menacing gestures, the savages fled. The next day, Samoset returned, bringing with him four others, who had a few skins and dried herrings, which they wished to exchange for other articles. It is somewhat remarkable that one of these Indians belonged to the company whom Hunt kidnapped and carried to Spain. There, with the others, being liberated from servitude through the agency of the monks of Malaga, he made his way to England, and finally got back to his own country! His name was Squanto. He was the only native left of those who had formerly occupied Patuxet, the place where the Pilgrims had fixed their settlement. Having been in England, he had obtained a smattering of the language, and could converse, though with difficulty, with the colonists. This party of four seem to have been a kind of advanced guard; for in the course of an hour, their great chief, Massasoit, made his appearance upon the top of a hill, accompanied by his brother Quadequina, and all their warriors. They came to visit the English. The two parties were at first somewhat shy of each other. But after sending messages to and fro by the interpreters, they cautiously came to a parley. Each party kept one or more of the others as hostages. After mutual salutations between Massasoit and Captain Standish, the chief was conducted to an unfinished house, where were placed for him a green rug and three or four cushions. Presently the Puritan governor advanced, in as great state as he could command, with a drum and trumpet sounding after him, and a few men with muskets, as a kind of body-guard. Salutations being over, which consisted of mutual kisses, they both took seats. "The governor called for some strong water, and drunk to him: and he drunk a great draught, that made him sweat all the while after." Meat was also offered to the chief and to his men, which was cheerfully received.

They then came to business. A treaty of friendship was entered into, in which they agreed to avoid mutual injuries, to deliver up articles belonging to their owners which might be carried off by the men of either party, and to leave behind them all weapons when they visited each other. It was further agreed, that if any nation made war upon the colonists, Massasoit should assist the English, and if any attacked Massasoit *unjustly*, the English would aid him; that if any of his people should hurt one of the colonists, he should send him to the colony for punishment, and that he should send to those tribes with whom he was in alliance information of this treaty, that they might be embraced in it also.

This was the first act of diplomacy executed in New England. Its negotiation occupied less than a day, and being of mutual benefit to both parties, it was strictly observed for more than fifty years. It was of importance to Massasoit to secure an alliance with the English, so as to have assistance in case he should be attacked by the powerful tribe of Narragansetts, who were his enemies. It was also of great moment to the English to be on friendly terms with neighboring Indians, who had it in their power to annoy them in various ways.

After Massasoit had left, his brother Quadequina came to the colonists, and was likewise received with marked distinction. He was afraid of the English guns, and at his desire they were carried away. He wondered greatly at the trumpet, and some of his men tried their skill at sounding it.

At the invitation of Massasoit, Captain Standish and Isaac Alderton visited him at his encampment. They were received with no sumptuous entertainment. All that he gave them were three or four ground nuts, and a little tobacco. By the request of the governor, he sent to the colonists his kettle, which they filled with peas, and gave him.

One fair day, Squanto went a fishing without pole, line, or hook. In the evening he returned with as many large, fat, "sweet" eels as he could lift with one hand. His method of catching them was to wade in the water, ascertain their beds with his feet, and, as they were in a torpid state in consequence of the cold, pick them up with his hand. He is supposed to have gone to a place which is now called Eel River, where large numbers are still caught every winter.

Such was the integrity of the Puritans, and their uniform obedience to the few laws which they had established, that no offence was committed among them till the latter part of March, when one John Billington was convicted of "contempt of the captain's lawful command and opprobrious speeches." The sentence which he received was peculiar. It was, that "he have his neck and heels tied together." The sentence, however, was not carried into execution. He humbled himself before the people, and asked for pardon. As this was his first offence, he was forgiven. Mercy, however, did not reform him. He continued to be a bad fellow. He was a profane, ungovernable, vicious knave, and finally came to a bad end. His eldest son, John, was of the same spirit with the father, and gave the colonists much trouble. On one occasion, he came near blowing up the Mayflower, by exploding squibs, and firing off a fowling-piece, when powder was strewed upon the floor, and a small cask of it was only about a yard from him. At another time, he wandered away from the colony, creating great anxiety, and subjecting them to the trouble of sending an expedition to find him. Billington senior was not a member of the church at Leyden. He came from London, and was in some way smuggled on board the Mayflower, without having any sympathy with the religious feeling of the Puritans.

The second offence committed was a duel between two *servants* of Mr. Hopkins. It was fought with sword and dagger. Both combatants were wounded. They were convicted, and sentenced "to have their head and feet tied together, and so to lie

5

for twenty-four hours without meat or drink." The cords were brought, their head and feet were tied according to sentence; but after lying about an hour, their sufferings were so severe that they began to beg for mercy. Their entreaties being seconded by their master, the governor, upon the promise of good conduct in future, released them. The promptness with which these three criminals were tried, convicted, and sentenced, and the forgiveness which they received, evinced the decision and the kindness of this early colonial government.

CHAPTER IV.

"Acquaintance I would have, but when 't depends
Not on the number, but the choice, of friends." — COWLEY.

"True happiness
Consists not in the multitude of friends,
But in the worth and choice: nor would I have
Virtue a popular regard pursue:
Let them be good that love me, though but few." — JONSON.

Plymouth in Summer. — Annoyance of Indian Loungers. — Visit to Massasoit. — Delivery of Presents. — The Message. — The Copper Chain. — Hard Lodging. — Subordinate Sachems. — Sports. — Shooting Fish. — Return of the Messengers. — Storm at Night. — Effect of the Visit. — Boy missing. — A Party sent after him. — Their Adventures. — Get News of the Boy. — Iyanough. — An old Squaw. — Her violent Passion. — Reason of it. — How she is pacified. — Indian Officiousness. — The Owner of the buried Corn found. — The lost Boy restored. — Natives rewarded. — Rumors of War. — Danger of the Colony. — Party suffer for Water. — Dance of the Squaws. — The Return.

WHEN the winter had passed away, and Nature had arrayed herself in her summer drapery, the colonists found that they had selected a pleasant spot for their settlement. The disappearance of ice and snow, the rich green of the hills and fields, variegated with numerous flowers, the forests covered with dense foliage, and the melody of birds in the groves, made Plymouth appear like a different country from that which they saw upon their first arrival. As the warm weather brought the Indians to the sea-shore for lobsters and fish, they were a great annoyance to the colony. The Pilgrims uniformly treated them with hospitality. This kindness furnished a motive for frequent visits, as the Indians would always go where they could get something to eat. The consequence was, that sometimes men, women, and children, in considerable numbers, were hanging around the village. Instead of turning them away, it was deemed best to send messengers to their great sagamore, Massasoit, state to him the grievance, and request him to issue orders prohibiting the annoyance. Another object which the colonists had in view in this embassage was, to compensate the Indians for the corn which they found upon Cape Cod on their first arrival. Stephen Hopkins and Edward Winslow received the appointment of ambassadors. Squanto, the Indian who had been kidnapped by Hunt, was to accompany them as interpreter. To secure a favorable reception for themselves and their message, they carried, as a present to the sagamore, a horseman's coat of red cotton, ornamented with lace, and a copper chain. When they arrived at Pokanoket, the residence of Massasoit, the sagamore was not at home. He was sent for, and soon made his appearance. The ambassadors saluted him by a discharge of their pieces, and were then welcomed in true Indian style by the chief. The first thing done after they had taken their seats was the delivery of the presents. When the chief was arrayed in the red coat, with the copper chain dangling from his neck, he and his men were highly gratified with his grand appearance. In the message which the ambassadors delivered, they informed the chief that his people had always been kindly received by the colonists, though they came very often and very many at a time; but as it was uncertain whether the corn which the English had planted would be productive, and as they had not much other food, they would be unable to extend to them the same hospitality in future which they had done, and which they would still be glad to do if it were in their power. They requested the chief, therefore, to interfere, and suffer none of his people to visit the colonists except those who had skins to trade. If, however, he desired to come himself, or had some particular friend who wished to see them, they would be pleased to receive him in the same manner as heretofore. That they might not be imposed by deceivers, the ambassadors requested the sagamore, whenever he should send any messenger to the colony, to give him the copper chain which had just been presented to him, and they would regard that as the credentials of his appointment, and would give credit to his message. They also related to Massasoit their discovery of the corn on the cape, and that they carried it away for their own use, with the intention, if the owners were ever found, of giving them ample compensation. They requested of him some seed corn to plant, so as to see which was best adapted to the soil of Plymouth.

After the message was delivered through the interpreter, Squanto, Massasoit replied, and consented to comply with their several requests. Business being over, the Indians lighted tobacco, gave it to the ambassadors to smoke, and entered into conversation respecting England and the king. So poor was the brave sagamore, that when the evening arrived, he had nothing to offer his distinguished guests for supper. In one part of the wigwam was a hard and rude looking bed made of plank, raised a few inches from the ground, and covered with a coarse, thin mat. When the visitors expressed a wish to sleep, one end of this plank platform was assigned them as their bed, whilst the chief, with his wife, slept at the other end. In addition to these four, two other Indians had to be accommodated, who, during the night, pressed so heavily upon the Englishmen, that their night's lodging was more wearisome than their days' journey. The visit of these strangers soon being rumored abroad, there came the next day many sachems, or subordinate chiefs, to see them. For their entertainment, the savages performed a number of their games, but were unwilling to shoot at a mark with the strangers for skins. About one o'clock, Massasoit, who had been fishing, returned, bringing with him two large fish, which he had shot. These were boiled, and portions of them were offered to the messengers. This was the first meal they had had for a day and two nights. The next day, very early in the morning, they left their poor, but friendly neighbors for home. They were heartily sick of Indian entertainment. The chief was sorry and ashamed that he could receive them in no better style. Friendship was in his heart, but abundance was not in his cabin. He did the best he could. On their return, the ambassadors were not only faint and hungry, but, to add to their trials, they were overtaken at night by a severe storm, accompanied with thunder and lightning. So violent were the wind and rain, that they found it impossible to keep their fire burning. The storm continued through the whole day; but they waded on with what little strength was left, until, after an absence of five days, they again reached Plymouth. The tendency of this visit was to strengthen the bonds of friendship existing between the Indians and the colonists.

It was probably a few days after this, that one of the boys belonging to the colony was missing.

Where he had gone, no one knew. His absence created great anxiety in the little community. Was he drowned? Had he been kidnapped by the Indians and carried into captivity? or had he wandered away and got lost? Various conjectures were indulged. A party of ten men were raised to go in search of him. They went in the shallop. They had not sailed far, before a heavy squall of wind, with lightning and rain, came down upon them with great force. A water spout was formed a short distance from them. They were in danger. Fortunately, it was of short duration. They passed the night in Cummaquid, now known as Barnstable Harbor. In the morning, seeing a couple of savages, they hailed them, and through their two interpreters, Squanto and another named Tokamahamon, made known who they were, and whom they were after. Very providentially, these Indians afforded great relief to the party, by the information that the lost boy was well, and might be found at Nauset, now called Eastham. At the invitation of the natives, six of the party went ashore, leaving, as hostages for their good treatment, four Indians in the shallop. They were introduced to their chief, Iyanough, a young man, not thirty years of age, of good personal appearance, courteous in his manners, and unlike an Indian, except in his costume. His entertainment was in harmony with his good appearance, being abundant and various.

At this place was a squaw, whom the colonists judged to be at least a hundred years old. As she had never seen an Englishman, she visited the party as a matter of curiosity; but when she saw them, she became greatly excited, giving indulgence to violent passion, and weeping excessively. The men were astonished. They knew not what it meant. They knew that they had done nothing to furnish occasion for such a development of strong feeling, and were at a loss to account for it. They asked the woman why she cried. She answered, that when Captain Hunt was here, she had three sons, who went on board of his vessel to trade, and that he carried them away captives to Spain, so that now she was cruelly deprived of their assistance and support in her old age. The Pilgrims sympathized with her in her distress, expressed great abhorrence of the conduct of Hunt, and told her that he was a bad man, and that all the English who had heard of his conduct in that affair strongly condemned it. As for themselves, they would not be guilty of similar conduct for all the skins in the land. To convince her of their sincerity, they gave her some presents, which served to allay her excited feelings. It will be remembered, that Squanto, one of the interpreters on this occasion, was also one of the number whom Hunt so nefariously kidnapped.

Having obtained track of the lost boy, they

hastened towards Eastham. Squanto was sent in advance to inform the chief of their approach and their errand. When they arrived at Eastham, they were greatly annoyed by the officiousness of the Indians, who surrounded the boat in great numbers, offering their help to get it in, as the water was low. The party were doubtful of their good intentions, as this was the place, and these the men, who made an attack upon them when they were examining the coast to find a desirable place for settlement. The boat soon got aground, and then the savages surrounded it in greater numbers than before. Among the Indians who were present on this occasion, was one to whom some of the corn belonged which the Pilgrims had found and carried away. They informed him that it had always been their intention to make restitution for it so soon as they found the owner, and that if he would visit the settlement at Plymouth, they would pay him for all they had taken.

Towards evening, their chief, Aspinet, came, accompanied by a large number of Indians, and what was more pleasing to the English, he brought with him the lost boy. Half of the Indians came up to the boat unarmed; the other half kept at a distance, with their bows and arrows ready, in case any occasion should occur for their use. One of the savages brought the boy through the water to the boat, and there he was delivered by the chief into the hands of the Puritans. It seems that for five days the boy had wandered over the hills and through the woods, living upon what few berries and fruits he could find. By that time, he reached an Indian settlement at Manomet, the present location of Sandwich. By the people there he was sent to the Nausets, where he was now found. When he was delivered to the colonists by Aspinet, the boy was decked in Indian tawdry style, having many beads hanging about him. Whether this was done in order to amuse the boy, or to please the English, we know not; probably the latter. The party rewarded the chief with a knife, which, no doubt, he highly prized, as their own knives were either stone or shell. They also gave a present to the Indian of Manomet, who first received the boy, and who had gone to the trouble of bringing him to Nauset. This boy was John Billington; a vicious lad, and a great plague to the colony.

Whilst the men were at Eastham, a rumor reached them that war had broken out between Massasoit and the Narragansetts, in consequence of an attack of the latter upon some of the men belonging to the former. They were alarmed. Being in league with Massasoit, they were bound to render him assistance, in case he had been attacked unjustly. Besides, they were apprehensive for the welfare of the colony, as the number of men there had been greatly reduced. Dr. Young, in his "Chronicles of the Pilgrim Fathers," says, that at the same time that these ten were on their excursion to Aspinet, "Winslow and Hopkins were absent on their expedition to Pokanoket, leaving only seven men at the plantation, the whole number surviving at this time being nineteen." If this were so, the settlement would have been in great danger in case it had been attacked by the enemies of Massasoit.

Massasoit and the Chain.

CHAPTER V.

> "The flying rumors gathered as they rolled;
> Scarce any tale was sooner heard than told;
> And all who told it added something new,
> And all who heard it made enlargement too;
> In every ear it spread, on every tongue it grew." — Pope

Startling Rumors. — Squanto reconnoitres. — Is taken. — Designs against him. — Supposed Murder. — A Party sent to Middleborough. — Midnight Attack. — Frightened Indians. — Squanto found. — Treatment of the Wounded. — Voyage to Massachusetts. — Origin of the Name. — Conduct of the Squaws. — The First Summer in Plymouth. — Preparations for Winter. — Colony alarmed. — Prepare to resist Invaders. — Pleasant Disappointment. — Arrival of the Fortune. — She brings no Stores. — The Consequence. — The Fortune returns. — Her Cargo and Capture.

The common proverb, that a story loses nothing by repetition, received confirmation in the present instance. By the time that the floating rumors reached the colony, whatever was their origin, they embraced the startling intelligence that the Narragansetts had invaded the domains of Massasoit; that Massasoit was either a prisoner, or had fled; that their interpreter, Squanto, had been cruelly murdered, and that some of Massasoit's men had revolted from their chief, and were striving to form a party in opposition to the English, and in violation of the league of friendship. Squanto had gone on a reconnoitring expedition, to obtain tidings, if possible, of Massasoit. Whilst lodging at Namasket, now called Middleborough, he was discovered by Corbitant, one of Massasoit's disaffected men. This fellow had expressed violent opposition to the alliance with the English, had given free use to contemptuous language against them, and had labored to poison the minds of others with similar sentiments. He was particularly bitter against Squanto, as he had rendered important service to the English in all their negotiations. "If Squanto were dead," said he, "the English would lose their tongue." He, therefore, with some of his evil disposed followers, came upon Squanto, surrounded the house in which he lodged, and took him prisoner. Squanto was accompanied on this excursion by another Indian, named Hobbamock. When Hobbamock saw that his friend was taken, and that Corbitant held a knife at his breast, as if to take his life, he made a violent effort, broke away from the enemy, and fled to Plymouth, with the news that Squanto was slain. Immediately the colony was in great commotion. Although they desired to live in peace with the Indians, they knew that it was not wise policy to allow offences of this kind to pass with impunity. Justice to themselves, to Squanto, and to Massasoit, demanded an immediate examination of the state of things, and a defence of their rights. Deliberations were held, and the conclusion reached, was, that, on the next day, a party of ten or twelve men should proceed to Middleborough, revenge the death of Squanto, take the sachem of the tribe prisoner, and retain him until they obtained tidings of their friend Massasoit. Accordingly, on the next day they departed, under the command of their champion, Captain Standish. The weather was rainy. They lost their way, through the mistake of Hobbamock, their guide, and the darkness of the night; but with the assistance of one of the others, who, fortunately, had been that way before, they found it again. Their plan was to come upon the house at midnight, surround it, and seize Corbitant before he could have time to escape. In the attack, they were to injure none except those who should attempt to flee. The plan being arranged, they made a supper in the dark of the contents of their knapsacks, and then threw them aside, to be free from their encumbrance. Each man having received his specific appointment, they passed cautiously and silently on, casting furtive glances in the deep gloom in every direction to avoid discovery. Presently they reach the house. Every man takes the place assigned him, and waits with a throbbing heart for the moment of attack. Those appointed to the service enter the house, and demand if Corbitant is there. The savages, aroused from their slumbers in the dead of night by a hostile party effecting an entrance into their cabin, are so thorougly alarmed as to be deprived of the power of speech. They are commanded not to stir at their peril. The whole family are aroused. Great excitement prevails. The guns of the invaders are fired at random. The whole town is in commotion. Some attempt to escape from the house through a private door, and are wounded. The women cling to Hobbamock, calling him "Friend, friend!" The boys, noticing that no injury is attempted against the women, cry out, "I am a girl, I am a girl." The invaders, in the mean time, endeavor to explain the object of their attack. They tell the people that they have come to revenge the death of their friend, Squanto, and want no one but Corbitant, his murderer. If he is not there, none shall be injured. After the fears of the Indians were allayed, and they had recovered their senses sufficiently to understand the explanation of this unexpected, nocturnal visit, they informed the invaders that Corbitant was not in the village, but that Squanto, whom they supposed he had murdered, was. Although the visitors were sorry to lose the former, they were greatly delighted to find the latter. In order to obtain full confirmation of this intelligence, they made the savages get up, strike a fire, and furnish a light, with which to search the house thoroughly. At the same time, Hobbamock ascended to the top of the house, and there called aloud for Squanto and Tokamahamon. In a few moments, they made their appearance, accompanied with others, some of whom were armed.

In the morning, the party visited Squanto at his own house, and breakfasted with him. They informed the Indians more fully of their determination to pursue Corbitant, and to contend with all others who should plot evil against the colony, or against Massasoit. They expressed regret that any of them had been wounded in the night's attack, but promised that if such would return with them to Plymouth, the physician would heal them. Two of the wounded, a man and woman, accepted their invitation.

About the middle of September, the colonists made their first voyage to Massachusetts, a word which signifies an arrow-shaped hill. This name is supposed to have been given to the surrounding country from the Blue Hills in Milton, which were formerly called Massachusetts Mount. They had interviews with the chief of a tribe in alliance with Massasoit, by whom they were treated with great kindness, and with some Indians of a hostile tribe, who, at first, were greatly alarmed; but as they discovered no evil intentions on the part of the visitors, they gathered courage to trade with them. Some of their squaws were so anxious to obtain the trinkets of the English, that they took off the garments which they wore, and sold them; and, as a substitute, tied leaves and branches about their persons. The party returned on the 22d, having been absent since the 18th.

During this first summer of their settlement, the Pilgrims were comfortably provided for. The weather was mild; their corn was productive; fish were obtained in considerable quantities; and later in the season, wild turkeys and venison were procured. As the cold weather advanced, they repaired their houses, so as to be the better able to endure the severity of the approaching winter. When it commenced, they were in health, and had "all things in plenty."

November 9, 1621, the colony was thrown into a state of great alarm, by intelligence received from an Indian that a vessel was seen approaching Cape Cod, which he believed to be French. As the English were not expecting the arrival of friends at that time, they also feared that the rumored vessel might be an enemy. When she came in sight, and made directly towards Plymouth harbor, their fears were strengthened. Agitation prevailed. No time was to be lost in getting prepared to give the intruder a warm reception. The governor gave command to fire a cannon, as a signal to those who were absent to hasten home. Immediately every male person in the colony who could shoulder a musket was on hand, armed and equipped with weapons and courage to repel the assailants, in case of an attack. We can imagine the painful suspense which they experienced as the vessel gradually approached. How intently they observed her! How carefully they studied her architecture, and the manner in which she was rigged! How they strained their eyes to make out her flag, the symbol of her nationality, that they might know with certainty what to expect, and what to do! Their suspense was not of long duration. As the vessel neared the harbor, they recognized her as a friend. It was the Fortune, bringing an accession of thirty-five persons from England to the colony. Fearful apprehension now gave place to great joy. There were warm greetings, rapid inquiries, brief answers. Painful and pleasurable intelligence was communicated in rapid succession, causing smiles and tears to alternate upon their features, like sunlight and shadow chasing each other over the fields.

Among those whom the Fortune brought over were Robert Cushman, and, in all probability, some of the others, of whom there were twenty, who were left behind with him when the Speedwell was abandoned.

As the friends in England had received from the colonists glowing accounts of the abundance of food which they found in the New World, this second company had deemed it unnecessary to bring with them any stores to be used after their arrival. This proved to be exceedingly unfortunate. Indeed, the vessel itself was furnished with supplies only to reach New England, so that the colonists were not only obliged out of their limited means to support the new immigrants, but also to furnish the vessel with stores for her return voyage. The consequence of this combination of unpropitious circumstances was, that soon after the departure of the Fortune, the colonists were all put upon half allowance of food, which, however, they endured with great patience.

The Fortune left Plymouth, on her return, December 13, 1621. She carried, as specimens of the productions of the country and of the industry of the colony, two hogsheads of peltries, consisting of beaver and otter skins, and a variety of lumber, the value of the whole being about $1500. As she approached the coast of England, she was discovered by a French vessel, pursued, overtaken, seized, and carried into France, where she was robbed of all that was valuable. After being detained there a fortnight, she and her crew were released.

CHAPTER VI.

"Treachery oft lurks
In compliments. You have sent so many posts
Of undertakings, they outride performance;
And make me think your fair pretences aim
At some intended ill, which my prevention
Must strive to avert."

Singular Visitor. — Mysterious Package for Squanto. — The Visitor made a Captive. — His Disclosures. — He is released and sent Home with a bold Message. — Squanto explains the Package. — A Package of Powder and Balls sent in Reply to it. — It is regarded with Terror. — Is finally sent back unopened. — Defensive Preparations. — First General Muster. — An Indian's Advice. — Another Expedition. — Signal for Return. — Why called back. — Hobbamock denies Indian Rumors. — Squanto falls under Suspicion. — His deceitful Conduct. — The buried Plague. — Massasoit demands Squanto's Death. — The Messengers ready to kill him. — His unexpected Deliverance. — The Messengers offended. — More Immigrants. — Winslow sent to Maine for Food. — Massacre in Virginia. — Fort built. — Used as a Church. — Puritan Character.

A SHORT time subsequent to the departure of the Fortune, an Indian from the Narragansett tribe visited the colony, as a messenger from Canonicus, their renowned chief. He inquired for Squanto, but seemed pleased when informed of his absence. Leaving for him a package of singular character, he was about to return immediately, but was prevented. This package consisted of a bundle of new arrows, wrapped in the skin of a rattlesnake. The governor having heard that the Narragansetts had threatened to make war upon the English, and being suspicious that arrows and rattlesnakes argued nothing friendly, that they could not be symbolical of the same sentiment as the olive branch, gave orders to Captain Standish to take the messenger prisoner, and detain him. At first, the poor fellow was frightened; but as his sentinels treated him with kindness, he gathered courage, and became communicative. In answer to inquiries, he informed the colonists that a messenger who had been sent to negotiate with them respecting a treaty of peace, the preceding summer, when he returned, had used his influence to persuade Canonicus to go to war. He also detained some of the presents which they had sent by him to his chief, and which, if they had been delivered to Canonicus, would have convinced him of their friendly designs, and prevented all belligerent threats. He said that when he should return and relate to Canonicus the real feelings of the English, he would enter into peace with them. The governor ordered him to inform his master that they had heard the many threats which he had uttered against them, and were offended; that although they were desirous of living on terms of peace with him, yet if he made any warlike demonstrations, he would find them prepared to meet him. Having concluded to release him, they offered him some food, which he declined receiving. He expressed much thankfulness for his deliverance. So great was his anxiety to return, that no persuasion, nor no violence of the weather, could induce him to tarry after his release. He set out for home in a driving storm.

When Squanto returned, and the package of arrows and snake-skin was placed in his hands, he said it expressed enmity, and was equivalent to a challenge. The question then arose, What shall we do ? How shall we reply to it ? After deliberation upon the subject, the governor filled the skin with powder and shot, and sent it back to Canonicus, with the message, that if the English were supplied with ships, they would save the Narragansetts the trouble of coming so far, by sailing to them and meeting them in their own dominions ; still, if they should come to the colony, they would always find the people ready to receive them. When this message was delivered to Canonicus, it impressed him with the courage of the English. He saw that threats did not terrify them. As to the snake-skin of powder and shot, under the influence of superstition, or fear, or perhaps both, he would not touch it, nor suffer it to stay in his house, nor in any part of his dominions. The messenger who brought it would not remove it. Another Indian took it up, and after it had been bandied about from one place to another, every where regarded as an object of terror, it was at last brought back, *unopened*, to the colony.

Notwithstanding the bold front which the English presented to the Indians, and their professed readiness to meet them, they were deeply sensible of their real weakness. They knew that the little town was illy prepared for a sudden or powerful attack. They accordingly adopted means of additional defence, by impaling it, including also the top of the hill under which the town was placed. They also made four bulwarks or "jetties" on the outside of the pale. The captain then divided his men into four companies, and appointed over each one to command. He also ordered a general training, when he assigned every officer his place, gave him his men, and charged them all to resort immediately, on any alarm, to their assigned places, under their own leaders. One part of the exercises on that occasion consisted in each officer marching his men to their appointed places, and there discharging their guns simultaneously. After this, the men escorted their officers to their dwellings, fired a salute in their honor, and then dispersed. This may be considered as "the first general muster in New England," and the germ of the militia system which at present prevails there.

After these arrangements were completed, it was

deemed desirable to make another voyage to the Massachusetts. Hobbamock endeavored to dissuade them from it, on the ground that he feared the Massachusetts were in league with the Narragansetts, and would seize the opportunity to attack, and, perhaps, kill the captain and his company during their absence, whilst the Narragansetts might, at the same time, make war upon the town. He also expressed the fear that the unsuspected Squanto was in alliance with them, and would employ every effort to entice the Pilgrims away from their boat, so that they might be more favorably attacked. It was, on the whole, deemed best, notwithstanding the statements of Hobbomock, to proceed on the voyage, though with more than usual caution. Accordingly, Captain Standish, with ten men, accompanied also by Squanto and Hobbomock, set sail. After proceeding a few miles, the wind ceased, and they were becalmed. Whilst they were lying here, they heard three reports of a cannon, as a signal fo. them to return. After they had left, an Indian who belonged to Squanto's family came running with great haste to some of the colonists who were at a distance from home, telling them to return immediately, as the Narragansetts, with Massasoit, Corbitant, and many others, were on their way to attack the settlement, during the absence of the captain. This story appeared the more plausible, from the fact that his face was covered with blood, which he said was occasioned by a wound that he received for speaking in defence of the colonists. He pretended to be in great fear, looking frequently behind him, as if to see whether he was pursued. Being brought to the governor, he told him the same story. The governor at once ordered the cannon to be fired, that if the voyagers were not beyond hearing, they might return. They retraced their course as soon as possible, with considerable anxiety to know the cause of their recall. Upon their arrival, they found the town prepared for action; but as soon as the rumor of the invasion was mentioned, Hobbamock said it was all false; that Massasoit was faithful to his treaty, and, besides, he would not go to war without his knowledge, as he always, on such occasions, consulted his braves, of whom he was one. To obtain certain information, the governor sent the wife of Hobbamock to Pokanoket, the residence of Massasoit, to make secret observations and inquiries, and bring back the result. Finding every thing peaceful at Pokanoket, she informed Massasoit of the rumor and its effect at the colony. The old chief was much offended at Squanto, but grateful to the governor that his confidence in him was not shaken, and repeated his determination to abide by the treaty. Squanto now fell under suspicion. The whole of this trouble was traced to him. He was severely reprimanded by the governor; but his services as interpreter being so important, he could not be dismissed. It was now ascertained to have been his policy to make the Indians around the settlement believe that he had great influence with the English, and that he could induce them to make war or peace. He would sometimes send word to the Indians that the English were about to attack them, in order that they might bestow upon him gifts to prevent it.

He was a deceitful, selfish, covetous, and ambitious fellow, and had managed his operations so artfully, as to be held in greater reverence by some of the Indians than Massasoit himself. Among the methods which he resorted to in order to impress the natives with the wonderful power of the English, was the relation of falsehoods respecting the miraculous agencies at their command. "These pale-faces," said he to a group of wondering natives, "are a wise and powerful people. Diseases are at their command. They have now buried in the ground, under their store house, the plague! They can send it forth to any place, or upon any people they please, and sweep them all away, though they themselves went not a step from home." When sent for by the governor, on one occasion, he with Hobbamock and several others entered the house. A hole had been dug in the floor for the purpose of concealing certain articles, and the ground was left in a broken state. Hobbamock, looking down to it, asked Squanto, —

"What does that mean?"

"That," said the wily Indian, "is the place where the plague is buried, that I told you of!"

Hobbamock, to be satisfied of the truth or falsehood of this marvellous statement, asked one of the colonists, on a subsequent occasion, if it were so.

"No," said the stern, truthful Puritan; "we have not the plague at our command, but the God whom we worship has, and he can send it forth to the destruction of both his enemies and ours."

When the true character of the interpreter became known, the colonists spared no pains to contradict his falsehoods, and to inform the natives of the true relations which he sustained.

The high-minded Massasoit was so indignant towards Squanto for the false rumors he had caused to be circulated respecting his alliance with the Narragansetts to oppose the English, that he desired to put him to death, and demanded him of the governor for that purpose. The governor replied, that although Squanto deserved death, yet it was desirable that he be spared, on account of his acquaintance with both languages, as, without him, it would be difficult for them to communicate with each other. Massasoit was not satisfied. He demanded him in accordance with the treaty which had been formed; yet, as a satisfaction to the governor, for the loss of his services, he offered him many beaver-skins. The governor replied, that the English did not give men to death for a reward, and therefore declined receiving his gifts. He, however, sent for Squanto, who, though he knew that the messengers were seeking his life, willingly complied with the command of the governor, and yielded himself up to his disposal. The messengers of Massasoit, being determined, if possible, to obtain Squanto, and having brought with them their sachem's knife for the purpose of cutting off his head and hands, continued to press their claims. The governor wavered. He had nearly decided to yield to the chief's wishes — he fully so decided, and just as he was about to deliver the poor, false interpreter into the hands of the messengers, which would have been the sealing of his doom, the giving of him over to the tortures of an Indian execution, an unexpected object seen in the distance thwarted his intentions.

This unexpected object was a boat, which was seen to cross the harbor, and conceal itself behind a headland, not far from the colony. It belonged not to the settlers, neither was it a native craft.

"May it not be French?"

"It is rumored that the French have combined with savages against us."

"Had we not better wait until this question is settled, before we deliver up Squanto?"

The governor so decided. When he informed the messengers of Massasoit that he would not deliver Squanto into their hands until he had ascertained the character of the suspicious boat, they were greatly enraged, and departed in a violent passion. This was a fortunate occurrence for the guilty interpreter. It resulted in his deliverance from death.

It was soon discovered that the boat which had produced this excitement was a friendly shallop, belonging to a vessel called the Sparrow, engaged in fishing on the coast of Maine. She was owned by Thomas Weston, a merchant of London, and had brought out six or seven passengers, to be landed at Plymouth. These immigrants, like those who came in the Fortune, brought no food with them. As it was now May, and the winter stock of the little colony nearly exhausted, as wild fowl could not be found, and they had neither hooks nor seines for fishing, there was a prospect of suffering in future, unless stores could be obtained from some unexpected quarter. It was concluded to send Mr. Winslow back with this shallop to Maine, to purchase, if possible, provisions from the fishing vessels which frequented that coast. He went, taking with him the boat belonging to the colony. He was kindly received by the fishermen, who, though they would not sell him victuals, cheerfully gave him all they could spare, expressing, at the same time, regret that they had not the ability to do more. He was successful in procuring enough to supply the wants of the colony, upon a moderate allowance, until their own crops were ripe.

Being informed by the captain of one of these fishermen, of a dreadful massacre of the whites by the Indians in Virginia, when three hundred and forty-seven were slain with great barbarity; and hearing, also, that the Indians round the colony were glorying in its weakness, and boasting how easily it could be destroyed, it was deemed advisable to erect a fort upon the top of the hill, under which the town was sheltered, from which a few individuals might make a vigorous defence. The work was commenced with great zeal, and with the unanimous concurrence of the whole company. After it was finished, it was used as a house of worship, as well as a place of defence! The Puritans believed in the importance of "works" as well as of faith. Their confidence in their heavenly Preserver was never suffered to diminish their efforts for self-preservation. They expected no Hercules to appear and remove their difficulties, so long as they did not put their own shoulder to the wheel. Sensible of their personal obligations, they adopted every possible means for their defence and prosperity, and then trusted in their divine Protector to crown them with success. The same building was at once their fort and their church. They went to prayer with their weapons on. They prefaced their battles with devotion. They rigidly kept the Sabbath, and they diligently worked six days in the week. They fished for a living, and fasted as an act of piety. They were thankful for blessings, and thoughtful in making bargains. They "walked softly before the Lord," and circumspectly in the midst of perils. They feared to offend God; but feared not to fight combined tribes of Indians when self-defence required it.

CHAPTER VII.

> "A lazy, lolling sort,
> Unseen at church, at senate, or at court,
> Of ever listless loit'rers, that attend
> No cause, no trust, no duty, and no friend." — POPE.

Arrival of the Charity and the Swan. — A New Colony.—Its Materials. — Its Object. — Its Difficulties. — An Expedition in Partnership. — Chatham. — Shyness of the Natives. — Success in Trade. — Squanto dies. — His last Request. — His History. — Favorable Providence. — Indiscretion of the New Colony. — Storm. — The Shallop aground. — Stores left in the Care of Indians. — The Return. — Puritan Firmness. — Indian Theft. — Restoration Demanded. — Its Result. — Ludicrous Ceremony. — Folly of Imitation. — Indian Gamblers. — Mysterious Visitors. — Their Object. — Indian Brawl and Murder. — Hobbamock's Advice. — A Powwow executed.

ABOUT the beginning of July, 1622, two vessels came round Cape Cod, and in a few hours anchored in the harbor of Plymouth. They were the Charity and the Swan. They belonged to Mr. Weston, who had formerly been much interested in the settlers at Plymouth, but who had recently concluded to plant a colony of his own somewhere in Massachusetts Bay. The pioneers of this new plantation had come over in these two vessels. They landed at Plymouth, and were received with as much hospitality as the impoverished condition of the colony would afford. They proved to be very undesirable visitors, and peculiarly unfit to be the founders of a settlement in the midst of hostile or suspicious Indians. They were a great annoyance to the Puritans whilst they tarried with them, and to the Indians after they left and had commenced a plantation of their own. They were a rude, profane, improvident, thievish set of men. They wasted the colonist's corn, and repaid their kindness with backbitings and revilings. An exploring party was sent out from them to discover a suitable place for settlement. They selected a spot which the Indians called Wessagusset, now known as Weymouth. Thither they all went except the invalids, who, by the permission of the governor, remained at Plymouth until they were restored to health. The kindness of the surgeon, Dr. Fuller, was shown in his making no charge for his professional services, although he might justly have sent in a bill.

This second colony was purely a business affair. It was a speculation. It was entirely destitute of every religious element, though it abounded with irreligious ones. The men were far from being Puritans, and ought never to be confounded with them. They feared neither God nor man. As might have been expected, they soon became embroiled with the Indians. The robberies and other crimes they committed irritated the savages, who poured their complaints into the ears of the Plymouth people. The Puritans remonstrated with them, told them of the wickedness of their course, and what would be its inevitable consequence if they persisted in it. At the same time, they informed the Indians that the two settlements were entirely independent of each other, and however much they disapproved the conduct of the Weymouthites, they could not control them, neither were they responsible for them.

In consequence of their mismanagement, it was not long before Weston's colony was reduced to great straits. It was therefore proposed, that, in company with some of the Plymouth people, they should make a voyage to the different Indian settlements along shore, in order to procure corn, beans, or other articles of food. Terms of agreement being settled between the two colonies, as to the division of the articles which they might obtain, the parties set sail in the Swan, taking with them the shallop. The first night they reached Manamoick, now known as Chatham. The governor, with Squanto and a few others, went ashore. At first, the natives were very shy. After they understood the object of the visit, they were more accessible. They welcomed the party in their usual rude style, furnishing them an abundance of venison and other food, but at the same time they were particularly careful to conceal from them their wigwams. It was evident that they were apprehensive of danger. They had not full confidence in the peaceful professions of their visitors. But when they learned that it was the governor's intention to spend the night on shore, they first had all their valuables removed from their huts and stored in some place of concealment, and then they invited the party to their homes. As one of the men walked about, he accidentally discovered their place of concealment; immediately the Indians fled, taking with them their property to hide in a place of greater security. Being discovered again, they fled as before, taking every thing with them. This they did repeatedly—as often as they were seen. Squanto finally succeeded in allaying their fears and persuading them to traffic. The party obtained from them eight hogsheads of corn and beans. This was the last service which poor Squanto rendered to the English. He was here attacked with a fever, attended with bleeding at the nose. His symptoms became worse. Nothing that was done produced any favorable effect. The disease hastened to a crisis. He was convinced that he could not recover. As memorials of his love and gratitude, he bequeathed various articles to his different English friends.

"Pray for me," said this dying Indian to Governor Bradford, "pray for me, that I may go to the Englishman's God in Heaven." After which he soon expired. This child of nature had passed through a more varied experience than usually fell to the lot of the sons of the forest. He had, as we have seen, been kidnapped by Hunt, taken across the Atlantic, and sold into slavery in Spain; — he was liberated by the Catholics; passed over to England; acquired something of the language; returned to the land of his fathers, and found himself the only one of his tribe in these parts who had not been cut off by the plague. His previous history had admirably qualified him to be an interpreter between the natives and the English, for in addition to his knowledge of the languages, his having been to England was of great importance, as it enabled him to give information to the Indians concerning the numbers, the ships, the cities, and the greatness of the English, by which they would have more correct and exalted opinions of them, and would more readily enter into alliance with them. Doubtless before the arrival of the Mayflower, Squanto had related his adventures to the Indians, and told them of the greatness and power of the English, as seen in their own land. It is not improbable that the information he gave was generally circulated among the tribes around Massachusetts Bay, so that they stood more in awe of the English than they would have done, if it had not been for his communications. It was certainly a very favorable providence that the Puritans, who, upon their arrival, were profoundly ignorant of the lan-

8

guage of the Indians, should so soon have found one competent to be an interpreter. Through his instrumentality, misunderstandings and difficulties were avoided, which otherwise might easily have occurred. The suspicions of the Indians were allayed. The real character and objects of the English were made known to them, and negotiations entered into which resulted in a friendly alliance.

It was the design of the party to visit some of the tribes to the south of Cape Cod. But, in consequence of the death of Squanto, this was abandoned. The wind being favorable, they returned to the Massachusetts, who had promised to plant a quantity of corn for the English. Upon their arrival there, they found the Indians suffering from the prevalence of a disease somewhat similar to the plague. Trade was destroyed there, in consequence of the indiscreet manner in which it had been conducted by Weston's men, they having purchased of the Indians at much higher rates than the Puritans were accustomed to give. Beads, trinkets, and cutlery had fallen in value. Notwithstanding their wickedness, they were not so good at a bargain as the Plymouthites. The Indians repeated their complaints of the villanies of the new colony. The party next visited Nauset, now Eastham, where they obtained eight or ten hogsheads of beans and corn. But a storm coming on, and their shallop being cast away, they had no means of removing the stores which they had bought. The corn was therefore placed in a heap, covered with mats and coarse sedge, and committed to the care of an Indian, with the promise, that, if he prevented it from being stolen, or from being injured by vermin, he should be suitably rewarded. The shallop was found half buried in the sand, but too much injured to be repaired with the means then at their disposal. They left that in the care of the chief, with the assurance, that, if it received no additional injury, and if the grain which they had purchased should not be touched, they would regard it as evidence of their sincere friendliness; but if the shallop or the stores should be molested, they would deem it an unfavorable indication, and would punish them accordingly. After the governor had completed these arrangements, he, with a portion of the company, set out for Plymouth, on foot, where they arrived safely, though with sore feet and great fatigue, after walking fifty miles.

Within two or three days after, the Swan arrived, bringing the remainder. The corn and beans which they had brought being now divided between the two parties, Weston's men returned home.

Whilst the Puritans were careful not to wrong the Indians, neither would they let the Indians injure them. They deemed it important always to exhibit a firm determination to exact their just dues, and by no means to be sinned against with impunity. When they detected, on the part of the natives, misdemeanors, their sachems were informed of it, and restitution demanded at once. An illustration of this decision of character was furnished during their recent visit at Eastham. An Indian entered their shallop, which had been drawn up into one of the numerous creeks with which that place abounds, and stole from it beads, scissors, and other articles. As soon as it was known, the captain took a number of his men, went to the sachem, informed him of the theft, and in a bold tone demanded the restoration of the missing articles, or the delivery of the thief, with the declaration, that, if this demand was unheeded, he would inflict summary punishment upon them before he left. He then withdrew till morning, declining to receive their proffered hospitality. The Indians not only knew that a robbery had been committed, but also who was the criminal. The next day, the sachem, accompanied with many of his tribe, visited the English, at their rendezvous, in as great state as he could command. As they approached the captain, each man thrust out his tongue the whole length, licked his hands from the wrists to the ends of his fingers, at the same time bending the knee and bowing in such an awkward, ungainly manner, that the English could with difficulty restrain their laughter. They presented an extremely ludicrous spectacle.

This ridiculous ceremony was not one of their own original customs. It was an attempt to imitate the English mode of salutation, according to instructions received from Squanto. As he had been to England, was acquainted with their language, and made it his home much of the time at Plymouth, where he saw their customs and manners daily, the Indians, without doubt, regarded him as fully competent to initiate them into the mysteries of English politeness. Hence their readiness to follow his directions on this occasion. But like certain imitations of foreign customs and fashions which are sometimes practised among civilized people, it partook of the absurd. However, it was well intended, and was received in the same spirit. Salutations being over, the sachem restored the stolen articles to the captain, at the same time informing him that he had given the guilty party a sound beating.

The Indians were great gamblers. In games of hazard or skill, they would sometimes lose their knives, hatchets, skins, clothes, dwellings, food, money, and even their own liberty. A vice seldom exists alone. Crimes are gregarious. As with more cultivated gamesters, so with these blacklegs of the forest, their playing sometimes led to quarrels, battles, wounds, and death.

One bitter cold January night, whilst the governor was at Buzzard's Bay, on a visit to the chief, Canacum, two Indians arrived from Manamoick, now Chatham. They entered the wigwam, deliberately laid aside their weapons, seated themselves by the fire, and took a pipe, without any words passing between them and the occupants of the tent. That they had come on some important embassy, was evident from their appearance and manners, but what it was no one knew. After remaining some time in silence, they ventured to raise their eyes towards Canacum. One of them gave a short address, and then, in the name of his sachem, presented to Canacum a basket of tobacco and a quantity of beads, which were thankfully received. He then disclosed the object of their visit in an address of greater length, the purport of which was as follows: As two men of their tribe were gambling, they fell into a quarrel. From words they came to blows, and in the fight one of them was slain! Unfortunately, the murderer was a powwow, a distinguished medicine man among them, whom they were reluctant to execute. But another tribe, more powerful than theirs, had espoused the cause of the murdered man, and had declared, that if the murderer was not put to death, they would deem it a just occasion of war, and would act accordingly. They had come, therefore, from their sachem, to obtain advice, as he had resolved to form no decision in the case until their return. After the speech, all the savages remained a considerable time in silence, as if solemnly considering the important subject. At length, they began to express their opinions. Hobbamock, who was present as the governor's interpreter, was asked his advice. He replied, that, as the acquittal of the powwow would lead to war, in which many would be killed, he thought it was better that one guilty person should die, rather than many who were innocent. Upon which, the murderer, who was then held in custody, was sentenced to be executed.

Gambling is a vice of a most enticing and destructive nature. It is painfully interesting to notice that it leads to the same dreadful results among the ignorant savages of the forest, as among professional gamesters of more civilized communities.

CHAPTER VIII.

"And when they talk of him, they shake their heads,
And whisper one another in the ear;
And he that speaks doth gripe the hearer's wrist;
Whilst he that hears makes fearful action,
And wrinkled brows, with nods, with rolling eyes." — SHAKSPEARE.

Fears of Conspiracy. — Illness of Massasoit. — Winslow, with two others, sets out to visit him. — Arrives at a Ferry. — Hears that Massasoit is dead. — Hobbamock's deep Grief. — His Description of the Chief. — They visit Corbitant's House. — A Messenger sent to Pokanoket. — Returns with the News that Massasoit is yet alive. — The Party press on. — Their Arrival. — Powwows at work upon the sick Chief. — Winslow prescribes for him. — He improves. — Eats too hearty, and becomes worse. — Indian Custom. — Efforts to persuade Massasoit to oppose the English. — They are unsuccessful. — Massasoit reveals the Conspiracy. — His Advice. — Conversation with Corbitant. — How the Puritans taught the Indians. — Origin of Traditions.

NOT long after this, the colonists began to suspect, from various facts which had come to their knowledge, that the Indians were plotting their destruction. These suspicions were afterwards confirmed, when it became necessary to take vigorous measures for their defence; but previous to any actual collision between them, the painful intelligence was brought to Plymouth, that Massasoit, their tried friend, was dangerously ill, and, also, that a ship belonging to the Dutch was stranded near his dwelling. It was deemed advisable for Winslow to visit him, to express the sympathy of the colonists in his affliction, and to render him any assistance in their power. Another object which they had in view, was to obtain an interview with the Dutch. As Winslow was somewhat acquainted with their language, he was selected for this purpose. He was accompanied on his journey by a Mr. John Hamden, a gentleman from London, who happened to be wintering at Plymouth, and who desired to see the country, and by Hobbamock, who, since the death of Squanto, had acted as interpreter for the colony. This was in March, 1623. The first night they reached Namasket, now Middleborough, where Standish and his men made their midnight attack in search of Corbitant. About noon, the next day, they arrived at a ferry; but seeing no one, Winslow fired his piece. This brought the Indians out, who informed him that Massasoit was dead and buried, and that the Dutch ship was afloat, and would probably be gone before they could reach there. This was unwelcome news, especially to the interpreter. They were now about three miles from the residence of Corbitant. As it was probable he would succeed to the chieftainship, upon the death of Massasoit, Winslow regarded it important to see him at that time, in order to enter into a more friendly alliance with him. As the others had no objection, although there was some peril in the undertaking, arising from the previous collision with Corbitant, he started towards Mattapoiset, his village. This was in Swansey. On the way, Hobbamock could not restrain his grief for the death of Massasoit, but gave utterance to his feelings in the exclamation, "O my chief, my dear, my loving chief! with many have I been acquainted, but none ever equalled thee." Then turning to his friend, he said, "O Master Winslow, his like you will never see again. He was not like other Indians, false, bloody, and implacable; but kind, easily appeased when angry, easily reconciled with offenders. He was reasonable in his requirements; was not ashamed to ask advice of those in low stations. He was a wise ruler. He governed better with mild, than other chiefs did with severe, measures, returning love for love. I fear you have not now a faithful friend left among the Indians." He would then break forth again in loud lamentations, "enough," as Winslow says, "to have made the hardest heart relent." There is something deeply affecting in the artlessness of this Indian's sorrow, and in the simple frankness of its utterance. It was not a mere outburst of feeling, for which no intelligent reason could be assigned, but a graphic delineation of the qualities of him whose decease was lamented, which delineation also served to deepen the intensity of his sorrow, by bringing more vividly before him the greatness of his loss. It reminds us of the lamentation of David over his friend Jonathan. "I am distressed for thee, my brother Jonathan: very pleasant hast thou been unto me. Thy love to me was wonderful, passing the love of women."

When they arrived at the residence of Corbitant, they found him absent. Upon making inquiries of his wife, they learned that she had not heard, with any degree of certainty, of Massasoit's death. They then hired a messenger, and sent him in great haste to Pokanoket, to ascertain the true state of the case. Just before sunset, he returned with the intelligence that the chief was not yet dead, but probably would be before they could arrive. They at once started, hoping to reach him before he breathed his last. When they arrived, they found the house so full of visitors, that it was with great difficulty they could effect an entrance. When they had succeeded, they beheld a scene so repulsive, and so annoying, as to be almost sufficient to banish what little vitality the poor, sick sagamore possessed. Not only was the place filled with filthy Indians, who effectually forbade all fresh air to the dying man, but the powwows were at work with their magical incantations, now rubbing him, now yelling, now making frantic gesticulations, so that if the disease had been intelligent, and cognizant of what was in progress, it would have been effectually frightened away. Six or eight were over him with their manipulations at once, and at a time when he ought to have been favored with perfect quiet. After their superstitious spells and exorcisms were over, they informed him that his English friends had come to see him. The visitors approached his couch, and rejoiced to find that his reason continued, though his sight was gone.

"Who is come?" asked the blind old chief. "Winsnow," said they, being unable to pronounce the *l*. "I want to speak with him," said the prostrate son of the forest, at the same time reaching forth his feeble hand. Winslow seized his extended hand, and placed himself close by his couch. "Art thou Winsnow?" feebly inquired the sick chief; "art thou Winsnow?" "Yes," was the reply. "O Winsnow, I shall never see thee more," said he, in his own language. Hobbamock was now called, and, through him, Winslow conveyed to the invalid the sympathy of the governor, informing him that such was his desire for his restoration to health, that he had sent him some things which he thought might be of service, and if he was willing to take them, he, himself, would prepare them. He said he was willing. Winslow then took upon the point of his knife a "confection of many comfortable conserves," which, with some difficulty, he passed between the patient's teeth. When this was swallowed, those that stood around him were filled with joy, this being the first that he had swallowed for two days. His mouth was found to be in a very bad state, and his tongue thickly coated, and greatly swollen. Winslow, with great kindness, washed his mouth, scraped his tongue, and cleansed him as well as he could. He then administered more of the conserves, which were swallowed with greater ease than the first. In a short time, he gave indications of decided improvement. Among other good signs, his sight began to return. As nothing suitable for a sick person could be found in his wigwam, a messenger was despatched to Plymouth to obtain medicines, chickens for broth, and other needful articles. This he regarded as extremely kind. Winslow, though unaccustomed to the business, made for him some broth without any fowl — a kind of mock-chicken soup. It was corn gruel, seasoned with green strawberry leaves and slices of sassafras root. He strained it through his pocket handkerchief, and then gave him about a half a pint, which he drank with a good relish. After this, he improved more rapidly. Being, as Hobbamock had said, a man of kindly feeling, he desired Winslow to visit some of his people who were sick, cleanse their mouths, and administer some of the same articles to them which he had given to him, "for," said he, "they are good persons." His request was complied with, though Winslow found it a very offensive service. He expressed a desire for some pottage made of goose, or duck. Winslow went out, in company with an Indian, after one. They discovered a brace of ducks. When Winslow, at a distance of more than a hundred paces, shot and killed one of them, his companion was astonished. It appeared to him almost miraculous. This was dressed and boiled. Being very fat, it made gross broth. Winslow was about to skim it. Massasoit forbade him. Winslow entreated him to allow it to be done, as otherwise it might injure him. The sick chief persisted in his refusal. When it was prepared, the invalid, instead of taking a small quantity, sufficient for his present wants, made a hearty meal. He overloaded his stomach, which, in the course of an hour, produced violent vomiting and bleeding at the nose, which continued for several hours. All now regretted that he had not complied with the directions of his nurse. His case became worse, and death seemed near. In the course of time, however, these unfavorable symptoms were allayed, and he began to improve. When the messengers returned from Plymouth, bringing with them chickens and medicine, he was so far recovered that he did not need the medicine, and the chickens he concluded to keep, in order to raise others.

It was customary among the Indians, when any one was sick with a disease that was not contagious, for all his friends to visit him, as a testimony of their respect and sympathy. So universally was the good prince of Pocanoket esteemed, that friends came from a distance of a hundred miles to see him, to whom he related all the circumstances of his illness; how blind he was; how extremely low; how his English friends visited him, nursed him, administered medicine, and raised him up to his present degree of strength. In this manner, the characteristic kindness of the Puritans became more widely known among the Indians who lived at a considerable distance from the colony. This served to impress them with the importance of being on friendly terms with the English, that they might receive similar favors.

It was stated at the commencement of our account of Massasoit's sickness, that the colonists were suspicious that evil was being plotted against them by the Indians. Winslow's visit to the chief resulted in obtaining more full and correct information upon this painful subject. The day previous to his arrival there, a certain sachem was with Massasoit, endeavoring to prejudice him against the English, and to obtain his consent to measures against them, which had been recently devised. He wanted the sick chief to unite with the unholy alliance which had been formed for their destruction. One of the arguments which this wily sachem employed, was that the English were not interested for the welfare of Massasoit; their friendship was hypocritical. If they really respected him, or cared for him, they would have visited him in his sickness; but as they had not, it proved that all their professions were hollow-hearted.

The next day, Winslow arrived as a messenger from the English, which disproved the false charges of the evil-disposed sachem. After his recovery, Massasoit was impelled by a sense of gratitude to disclose to the English the conspiracy which had been formed for the purpose of extirpating both colonies. Through Hobbamock, he revealed that the Massachusetts, and the Indians of the several places now known as Eastham, Cape Cod, Falmouth, Barnstable, Buzzard's Bay, Wareham, and Martha's Vineyard, had entered into combination for that object, and he had been strongly urged to join, but had refused to have any thing to do with the murderous affair. He also advised the English, as the best course they could pursue, to put to death the Indians of Massachusetts, who were the authors of this plot, and then it would be destroyed. He earnestly charged them to communicate fully this information and advice to the governor.

As the Dutch ship, which had been aground, was

gotten off, and had left before Winslow's arrival, nothing more remained for him to do. He therefore departed.

On his return, he spent the night at Swansey, with Corbitant, whom he says he found to be "a notable politician, yet full of merry jests and squibs, and never better pleased than when the like are returned again upon him."

"If I were sick, as Massasoit has been," asked he, "and should send word to Plymouth, would Mr. Governor send me medicine?"

"Yes."

"Would you bring it to me?"

"Certainly," said Winslow.

At this he was highly delighted, and expressed many thanks.

"How did you dare," said he again, "to go so far into the country, being but two of you?"

"Because, where there is true love," answered Winslow, "there is no fear; and my heart is so upright towards the Indians, that I am not in the least degree fearful to go among them."

"If you love us so much," continued the shrewd Indian, "how happens it that when we visit Plymouth you stand upon your guard, and present the mouths of your guns towards us?"

"Because that is the most honorable reception

we can give you. It is in that way that we salute our most distinguished guests."

Corbitant shook his head, as if in doubt, saying, "I don't like such salutations."

Having noticed, that before their meals they asked a blessing, and afterwards returned thanks, he asked them why they did it. This led to a long conversation upon the character and works of the Deity; upon the relations which men sustain to him as their preserver and constant benefactor, and the duties which they owe to him as such, with which he and others who were present were pleased. When the Ten Commandments were repeated, they approved of all except the seventh. They thought there were many objections to "tying a man to one woman." They wanted, as many do at the present day, greater liberty.

This is a specimen of the manner in which the Puritans endeavored to communicate religious truths to the minds of these ignorant and degraded savages. When among them, they observed religious services at their meals. Neither fear nor pride prevented them. They also continued the practice of morning and evening devotions. They strictly regarded the Sabbath, and when opportunity presented, especially by inquiries from the savages, they imparted, in a familiar manner, the elementary truths of the Bible. As they became better acquainted with each other, and could converse more easily, many such conversations as the above were held. The truths and scriptural facts which were in this way imparted to a few, would by them be communicated to their whole tribe, and would be made topics of discussion among them. It is not improbable, that in this manner some of the more prominent truths of the Bible became widely disseminated among the natives of the continent. As those who first learned them were scattered abroad by war, or pestilence, or for want of good hunting grounds, they would, in their intercourse with others, give them still wider diffusion. After the lapse of years, these truths might, especially among tribes at the greatest distance from the settlements, assume the character of traditions, and, as such, be handed down to their posterity. Traditions which now exist among some of the Indians of the remote West, and which bear a close analogy to Scripture history, may have originated in this manner.

After spending the night with Corbitant, and having hospitable and pleasant entertainment, they bade him adieu, and passed on towards Middleborough. Here they spent the second night. The next day they arrived at home.

CHAPTER IX.

"O Conspiracy!
Sham'st thou to show thy dangerous brow by night,
When evils are most free? O, then, by day
Where wilt thou find a cavern dark enough
To mask thy monstrous visage? Seek none, conspiracy;
Hide it in smiles and affability." — SHAKSPEARE.

Condition of Weston's Colony. — Man drowned in digging Clams. — Indian Policy. — The Men rob them. — Indians complain. — A slanderous Tradition. — Butler perpetuates it. — Its Origin. — Plymouth not responsible for Weymouth. — Consultation of the two Colonies. — Sanders goes to Maine for Provisions. — Dangers of the English. — Their Perils considered by the Court. — Standish sent to Weymouth to capture Indians. — His Instructions. — Insulting Conduct of the Indians. — Pratt's providential Escape. — He relates the wretched Condition of Weymouth. — Pratt is pursued. — His Pursuer captured as a Spy. — Standish arrives at Weymouth. — Makes known the Conspiracy. — The Captain's Policy. — Indians pretend they know his Object. — Their Insults. — The boasting of Indian Braves. — The Forbearance of the Captain.

THE planting of Weston's colony at Weymouth proved an unfortunate affair. It was composed of bad materials, and managed without tact, judgment, or prudence. The men were indolent, vicious, and destitute of public spirit. Their supplies were soon exhausted, and, by the end of February, 1623, they were reduced to great distress. They then degraded themselves to become "hewers of wood and carriers of water" to the Indians, for a meal's victuals, when; with ordinary industry, employed in other directions, they might have supplied themselves far more abundantly.

So reduced in strength had the men become, in consequence of the want of food, that one of them, who was engaged in digging clams, sunk in the mud; and being unable to extricate himself, was overwhelmed by the rising tide, and drowned.

The Indians knew the weakness of the Weymouthites, and, on account of the servile services they had received from them, they regarded them with contempt. To reduce them to still greater straits, they refused to lend or sell them any corn, beans, or bread, on any terms. The men resorted to theft. When they found any of the hiding-places where the Indians concealed their grain, they dug it up, and appropriated it to their own use. The Indians complained and threatened. To appease them, some of the criminals were whipped and placed in the stocks. As this neither produced amendment, nor pacified the natives, more severe measures were resorted to, and one of them was hung. A tradition has become current, that at this execution, a sick, feeble, and worthless old man, who could have rendered no aid to repel an attack of the Indians, was substituted in the place of the criminal, who was a strong young man, and might be of great service to the colony in time of war.

As the execution was mainly to satisfy the Indians, it was argued that one person would answer as well for that purpose as another, so long as the savages were deceived, which might easily be effected by dressing the innocent sick person in the clothes of the criminal. The Indians would then suppose that the guilty person was on the gallows. Unfortunately, this tradition has been widely circulated, and rendered immortal by Butler, in the following lines of Hudibras: —

> "Our brethren of New England use
> Choice malefactors to excuse,
> And hang the guiltless in their stead,
> Of whom the churches have less need;
> As lately happened."

It is proper that this base slander should be denied. We have not seen a particle of evidence that such a shameful transaction ever took place. The first writer who alludes to it mentions it simply as a suggestion that was made at the time, but which *was rejected.* The nearest approximation to evidence of such an occurrence is the statement of Mr. Hubbard, that the person executed was really guilty, as were many of the others; "yet it is possible that justice might be executed, not on him that most deserved it, but on him that could best be spared, or who was not likely to live long, if he had been let alone." But even this language does not convey the idea, that after one person had been convicted, another one was executed in his stead; but only, that of the many criminals, the most guilty one might not have been selected for trial and condemnation. Yet the one who was tried and condemned was the one who was executed, and whose guilt is admitted. But even if it were otherwise, and the unjust substitution had taken place, the Puritans are not to be censured. They were nowise connected with the affair, and seem not to have been informed of it until it was over, when the intelligence was communicated by a messenger from Weymouth. The two colonies were entirely independent of each other. The Puritans at Plymouth were in no sense responsible for the deeds of the other settlement. Butler errs in calling them "our brethren of New England." They were not Puritans. We have no evidence that they had a church, or that any of them were members of a church; and nothing that they did should be allowed to injure, in the least degree, the reputation of the Pilgrims.

When the settlers at Weymouth found it impossible to obtain any thing from the Indians with their consent, they resolved to supply their wants by taking forcible possession of their stores. To this end they closed up every entrance to their town, except one, and strengthened the defences which they had built. Before entering upon their foraging expedition, which would be equivalent to a declaration of war, they consulted with the leading men at Plymouth.

They narrated the conduct of the Indians, the painful straits to which the colony was reduced, and the absolute necessity of their procuring supplies. They then disclosed their intended attack, and asked their opinion. After giving the matter their serious consideration, the Puritans expressed the opinion that the contemplated movement would be untimely, impolitic, and dangerous; that it would be a violation of the law of their king, and of the law of God; and they presented a variety of forcible reasons to dissuade them from its execution. This judicious advice they resolved to comply with for the present. Their next measure was to send their overseer, Mr. John Sanders, to the coast of Maine, for provisions. The friends at Plymouth supplied him with corn for his voyage, on which he set out in the latter part of February.

After his departure, additional evidence was discovered of the conspiracy among the Indians. It was more fully divulged by some of the Indians themselves. Dangers thickened around the English. They were so few and weak, in comparison with the neighboring tribes, that if there had been a sudden, simultaneous, and courageous attack, on the part of the savages who had joined the plot, they would easily have annihilated both settlements. This the English knew. They were aware, also, that no time was to be lost; that whilst they were deliberating, the war whoop might ring in their ears, and their hearth fires be quenched in blood. At the annual meeting of the General Court, which soon occurred, the whole subject was submitted by the governor to that body. They referred it to the governor, his assistant, and the captain, with such others as they might be disposed to consult. This committee were empowered to devise and execute such measures as the exigency seemed to them to demand. The conclusion to which this committee came was, that Captain Standish should take as many men as he thought necessary for the purpose, and proceed to the Massachusetts, ostensibly for trade. After making Weston's colony acquainted with the bloody conspiracy which had been formed against the English, and the real object of this visit, Standish was then to open trade with the Indians, and carefully observe all their demeanor; but he was to avoid, if possible, an actual collision, until an Indian by the name of Wituwamat was in his power, whom he was to kill, and then send his head to Plymouth. This fellow was selected as a victim, because he was a notorious, insulting villain, whose conduct had previously been extremely aggravating. He had boasted in a pompous and irritating manner of having shed the blood of both English and French, whom he derided for want of courage, saying that "they died crying, making sour faces, more like children than men." On a former occasion, when Captain Standish was at Manomet, this fellow endeavored to persuade Canacum, the sachem of that place, to destroy him, as he then had a fair opportunity, stating to him that the Massachusetts, in order to secure their own preservation, had combined to cut off Weston's colony, but had concluded to delay until they were strong enough to destroy Plymouth also. As he now had the captain in his power, it was a good time to put him and his company out of the way.

In consequence of his known enmity to the colonists, and of the threats which he had used, it was considered important to the safety of the settlers that he should be slain. Hence the instructions to the captain to avoid an attack until Wituwamat was in his power.

The captain took only eight men with him on this perilous expedition. He thought that a larger number would excite suspicion among the Indians of their conspiracy being detected. Before he set out, a messenger by the name of Pratt arrived at Plymouth, from Weston's plantation, with a pack on his shoulders, bringing information that the state of things there was worse than ever. The men were reduced to the extremes of poverty, having been obliged to sell their clothes for food, and now, being unable to go in pursuit of food on account of their nakedness, they were perishing from cold and famine. If at any time they obtained victuals, the Indians were so strong and bold that they would enter their houses, take it from the pot where it was being cooked, and in a tantalizing manner would eat it before their eyes. If they remonstrated, the savages would put a knife to their breasts and threaten their lives. One of the colonists had abandoned his companions and turned savage; the most of the people had forsaken the town, and made their rendezvous wherever they happened to find food. They had separated into three companies, very few of them having any powder or shot with which to procure game or defend themselves if attacked. What would be the ultimate result he knew not. Being afraid to tarry there any longer, he had set out, although he knew not the way, to come to Plymouth and ask the privilege of remaining there till affairs became more settled.

Soon after this man had left the Massachusetts, at Weymouth, the Indians missed him, and suspecting that he had gone to Plymouth, they immediately sent a messenger in pursuit of him, probably with orders to put him to death; as they expressed the opinion he would never reach Plymouth, but would be devoured by wild beasts on the journey. Guided by a kind Providence, Pratt lost his way; so that the Indian in pursuit, who took the usual route, missed him, and thus his life was saved. The Indian passed by Plymouth on his way to Buzzard's Bay. When he returned he stopped there, pretending to make a friendly call, but in reality to observe their condition, and see whether they were reduced to the poverty and helplessness of Weston's people, which he hoped was the case; the intelligence of which, he knew would be glad tidings to the Massachusetts. The governor immediately arrested him, and kept him a prisoner. He was sent to the fort and chained to a staple, where he was informed he must remain under guard until Standish returned from his expedition against his tribe. This must have been evil tidings to the poor captive spy, who knew that his own people were only waiting for a favorable opportunity to pounce upon the colony like a vulture upon its prey, and who, by his present captivity, had abundant reason to believe that their conspiracy was detected, and would be punished.

After Pratt's relation, Standish, with his small company, proceeded to Weymouth with all speed. When they arrived, seeing the ship which was connected with the colony in the harbor, they went on board to have some consultation as to the best measures to be adopted with reference to the approaching crisis. Finding no one on deck, they entered the cabin. No one was there! They examined other parts of the vessel, and to their great surprise found it entirely forsaken — not even one person left as guard. What did it mean? Had the crew been slain by the Indians since Pratt left? Appearances did not favor such a conclusion. No weapons were about, as if left in haste; no marks of blood were seen. Had they then been seized and taken into captivity? To ascertain whether they were in the neighborhood, one of the men on board fired a musket. Immediately the overseer and several of his companions presented themselves upon the shore. They were there for the purpose of gathering ground nuts and other articles to eat. After salutations were exchanged, Captain Standish asked, —

"How do you dare to leave your ship, and live in so much security?"

"O," replied they, utterly insensible of their perilous condition, "we have no fear of the Indians, but live with them and suffer them to lodge with us, without our having a gun or sword, or even needing one."

"Well, well," said Standish, "if you have no occasion for vigilance, so much the better. But where are those whom Mr. Sanders left in charge of affairs during his absence?"

"They are at the plantation." Thither the captain went. He informed them of the Indian conspiracy, and that the object of his visit was to cut off the ringleaders. He also invited them, if they were so disposed, to reside at Plymouth, until this dark cloud had passed away, and they were placed in circumstances more favorable to their prosperity. But if they thought it advisable to pursue any other course, he would assist them to the extent of his ability. The men now had their eyes opened. They were surprised at their own previous blindness. They could call to recollection various circumstances which had occurred in their intercourse with the natives, which were in keeping with the conspiracy. They acknowledged that it was all of divine mercy that they had not been slain before the captain's arrival. They desired that he would proceed at once to the accomplishment of his object. He enjoined upon them the observance of the greatest secrecy, that the Indians might not discover their intentions.

He also advised them to send orders to that third of the company who were at the greatest distance from the plantation to return, and, on pain of death, to keep the town, promising to supply, from his own stores, each man with a pint of corn a day. Some time elapsed before any active measures were adopted, in consequence of storms and rain. During this delay, an Indian visited the plantation, bringing some skins, professedly to trade. In reality he was a spy, whose object it was to obtain, in a covert manner, what information he could respecting the suspicions and plans of the English. The captain endeavored to appear perfectly friendly and unsuspecting, yet when the spy returned, he reported that he saw from the captain's eyes that there was anger in his heart. The Indians, therefore, thought that their conspiracy was detected. But, instead of retreating beyond the reach of the English, until their arrangements with the other tribes were consummated, they put on a bold front, visited the plantation frequently, and even expressed the belief to them that their object was to slay them. One of their braves, whose name was Pecksuot, a man of courage, but at the same time a braggadocio, went to Hobbamock, who was with Standish as his interpreter, and told him that he had been informed that the captain had come to "kill himself and the rest of the salvages." "Tell him," said he, "we know it, but we neither fear him, nor will we shun him; let him attack us when he pleases, he shall not take us by surprise." These were courageous words for one who had reason to believe that his plots were discovered. He was probably emboldened by his confidence in the success of the conspiracy. The Indians who had entered into the alliance were so numerous, and the colonists so few and feeble, that success seemed to them almost a certainty. Hence, these insulting savages would sometimes come to the plantation alone, or several together, and, placing themselves in the presence of the captain, would whet their knives, sharpen their points, and make various gestures and speeches of an insulting nature, as if on purpose to irritate him to some deed of blood. Wituwamat was not wanting on these occasions. He boasted of the fine qualities of his knife, on the handle of which was pictured a woman's face; "but," said he, "I have another at home with which I have killed both French and English, and that hath a man's face on it; and by and by these two must marry." Not long after, when speaking of the knife he then had, he said, "By and by this shall see, and by and by it shall eat, but not speak;" as if alluding to some intended murder which his knife would commit silently, whilst the muskets of the English always *reported* their doings. Pecksuot was a man of large size and great muscular strength, while Standish was comparatively small. On one occasion he said to Standish, —

"You are a great officer, but a little man; and though I am no sachem, yet I am a courageous man, and possess great strength."

All these things the captain endured with much forbearance. His determination was fixed, and his plans formed ; he was only waiting a suitable opportunity for their execution. He wisely resolved that no insults of the savages should betray him into premature movements. Like the lion, with his eye fixed upon his prey, he calmly waited for a favorable moment of attack. It was not long before this arrived.

CHAPTER X.

> "See, his face is black and full of blood;
> His eyeballs farther out than when he lived;
> Staring full ghastly, like a strangled man;
> His hair upreared, his nostrils stretched with struggling;
> His hands abroad displayed, as one that grasped
> And tugged for life, and was by strength subdued." — Shakspeare.

A silent, but fearful Massacre. — Hobbamock compliments Standish. — Women held Captives. — An Indian escapes. — Three Englishmen among the Indians. — The Indians haste away at Midnight. — They meet Standish and his Men. — A Skirmish. — The Indians defeated. — Hobbamock's Bravery. — The Indian Women released uninjured. — The Puritans responsible for the Massacre. — Their Apology. — A young Indian's Confession. — Standish returns, taking an Indian's Head. — The captured Spy recognizes it. — The Spy released and sent as a Messenger. — A Squaw brings back an Answer. — The three Englishmen killed. — The Terror of the Natives. — They attempt to send a Peace-offering to the Governor. — The Boat is wrecked. — Robinson's Letter.

On the day following the conversation which we gave at the close of the last chapter, a combination of circumstances seemed to indicate to Standish that the favorable moment for the execution of his plans had arrived. Pecksuot, Wituwamat, with another Indian, and a young villain about eighteen years of age, brother to Wituwamat, who had played many scurrilous tricks upon the more feeble of the colonists, were together in one house; there were also present about the same number of the

English, with Hobbamock. The door being made fast, Standish gave the signal for the dreadful work of death to be commenced. Each man chose his victim, and the fearful struggle began. Standish selected the insulting braggadocio, Pecksuot, and snatching the knife from his neck, which he had impudently sharpened in the captain's presence, he plunged it in his heart's blood! One blow was not sufficient. The Indian resisted. He was wounded again; he endeavored to recover; his eyes glared; he snatched violently after his knife, but failed to get it; he fought with the energy of despair: the struggle was terrific, but brief. In a few minutes, the boastful warrior ceased to breathe. He had whetted his knife for his own death. At the same time, similar conflicts were in progress between Wituwamat and an Englishman, and the other Indian and a colonist. They knew that all flight was impossible. There was no quarter asked nor offered; one of each couple must die; one or the other party must be exterminated. They fought with desperation to the very last. There were no shrieks, no cries, no war whoops; nothing but a deadly struggle. Their silence rendered the contest more awful. A shriek would have been a relief. In a few minutes, all the savages were dead except the youth. He was reserved to be hanged. During all this time, Hobbamock was a silent spectator of the tragic scene. He took no part with either. After it was all over, he said to Standish, whilst a smile played over his features, "Yesterday, Pecksuot, bragging of his own strength and stature, said, though you were a great captain, yet you were but a little man; but to-day, I see you are big enough to lay him on the ground." But Standish desired not his praise; he was intent upon the overthrow of the conspirators. Some Indian women who were at Weymouth he committed to the custody of Weston's people, for safe keeping till further orders. He then sent a messenger to another company of the men, with instructions for them to kill all the Indians who were with them. They slew two. Standish and a few others went to another place, and killed one more. It was the captain's design to have kept all this concealed from the natives; but his purpose was defeated, through the negligence of one of the men in suffering an Indian to escape, who immediately disclosed these massacres to the tribe.

A short time previous to this tragic adventure, three of Weston's men had gone and offered to build canoes for the sachem of one of the tribes in the neighborhood, where they had formerly been well fed, when performing similar service. The first night of their arrival, at a late hour, a messenger came, almost breathless, perhaps the one who had escaped from Weymouth, who delivered, in his own language, a short message. What it was, the Englishmen knew not. That it was of great importance, was evident from the conduct of the Indians; for no sooner was it delivered, than a general excitement was produced. The Indians arose, hastily dressed themselves, seized their bows and arrows, gathered together for a few moments' consultation, and then, telling the English that they were going a hunting, and would return with plenty of venison, they hastily departed.

The oldest and most experienced Englishmen present thought that this midnight manœuvre augured nothing good. Viewing this conduct of the Indians in connection with the strict charge of Standish, that none of the men should leave the plantation, he feared that a collision had, or would soon ensue. He proposed to his companions to return. They unwisely refused. He set out, therefore, alone. To avoid discovery, in case of pursuit, he shunned the paths, and groped his way in the darkness, through the unbroken fields and forests, by which means he successfully escaped.

After the massacre at Weymouth, the captain took half of his own men, with one or two of Weston's party and Hobbamock, and went forth to plunder the Indians. After marching some distance, they met a party of the natives coming towards them — probably those who had left home so suddenly at night. Each regarded the other as on a belligerent expedition. A hill being near, the possession of which would give advantage in the fight, both parties endeavored to obtain it. Standish was successful. The Indians then ran, according to their usual custom, and, concealing themselves behind trees, rocks, and bushes, let fly a shower of arrows, aimed especially at Standish and Hobbamock. The combativeness of Hobbamock was now excited. He threw off his coat, and dashed in among them with great bravery. The savages, knowing him, retreated. Hobbamock pursued. The English could not keep up with him. These latter, seeing the arm and half of a face of a notorious character in the act of drawing his bow at Captain Standish, two of them fired at him, and broke his exposed arm. The Indians retreated to a swamp. The captain endeavored to hold a parley with them. They returned insulting language. He then challenged the sachem to show himself and fight openly like a man, and not get behind trees, and use hard words, like a cowardly squaw. His challenge and ridicule were alike unheeded. The sachem and his men fled, leaving the English victorious. The captain then returned to Weymouth. The Indian women who were there he released without any injury. He would not even allow the men to take from them their beaver garments, nor in any way to insult them. We cannot but admire his scrupulous regard for the helplessness and delicacy of the female sex.

In order to screen the Puritans from the responsibility of this massacre of the Indians at Weymouth, it will not do to say that Standish was not a member of the church, and, therefore, was no more of a Puritan than the men of Weston's colony; that he was merely a military officer, and in this campaign against the enemy, was governed by ordinary military usages; for, admitting that all this was true, it must not be forgotten that he had received special instructions from the proper authorities at Plymouth how to proceed, and had simply executed those instructions. He was their servant, and had done their bidding; they were, therefore, responsible for his deeds.

The best justification of the act must be based upon the perilous condition in which the English were then placed. They knew their own weakness; they were aware of the existence of a powerful conspiracy against them; they had received intelligence of the dreadful massacre by the Indians in Virginia. No time was to be lost. The savages might come down upon them with the suddenness and terribleness of an Alpine avalanche. It appeared to them essential to their safety, that they should take the initiative in the approaching conflict; that by some bold and severe stroke, they should send terror among the Indians before they were generally aware of the discovery of their conspiracy. In forming our opinion of the morality of their conduct in this trying crisis, we must have some regard to the sentiments which generally prevailed among Christian people at that time, respecting the lawfulness of defensive war.

After the massacre, a young Indian, who was of a mild, amiable, and confiding disposition, although he knew of the death of his countrymen, came fearlessly to the captain, professing love and good will, and honestly confessed that the Indians had resolved to murder Weston's colony so soon as two more canoes were finished, which Weston's men were making for them at the time of the outbreak, and with which they intended to have taken their ships.

Weston's people were now thoroughly tired of the new settlement. It had proved a failure, and they were resolved to abandon it. Some of them were desirous of going to the coast of Maine, with the hope of finding a passage to England in some of the fishermen which resorted there. Standish furnished them with corn to reach the coast, which so reduced the little quantity he had, as to leave him hardly enough to last till he could return home. Others of them preferred to go with him to Plymouth, as they did not want to associate with those who were going to Maine. After the former party had sailed and cleared the bay, Standish took the others in his shallop and returned victoriously to Plymouth, where he was received with great joy.

He did not fail to obey the command of the governor to bring back with him the head of one of the prominent conspirators. As an object of terror to the Indians, it was set up in a conspicuous place in the fort.

The Indian who pursued Pratt, but failed of overtaking him, was left, it will be remembered, a prisoner at Plymouth. When the bloody trophy of the captain was shown him, he was asked if he knew whose head it was. He looked mournfully upon it, and said, "Yes; it is Wituwamat's." He also confessed the conspiracy, and said that his chief was urged to it by his men, among whom five were more urgent in pressing him into it than the others, two of whom, Pecksuot and Wituwamat, were slain. The other three were medicine men, or conjurors. He denied being implicated in it himself. He said he did not belong to their tribe, but was a stranger among them, and earnestly entreated the colonists not to put him to death. Hobbamock interceded for him, and gave him a good character, though it afterwards appeared that he was induced so to do by the influence of a bribe.

The Puritans were not revengeful. The shedding of blood afforded them no pleasure. Hence they had no disposition to execute the unfortunate native who was now in their power. Having recently been so victorious, they could afford now to be generous. Besides, by sparing his life and sending him home, they could forward a message to his chief which might prevent the necessity of further bloodshed. He was accordingly released and brought before the governor, who charged him, through Hobbamock, the interpreter, to say to Obtakiest, the chief of the Massachusetts Indians, that the Puritans would not have attacked them if they had not been compelled to by their own treachery, and therefore the conspirators were to blame; that if he entered into another similar plot, they would drive him from his country, and utterly extirpate his tribe; of this he was now fairly warned; and also that he must send back the three Englishmen he had, and not slay them; that he must not injure what is left of the plantation at Weymouth; and that this messenger must come back with the English, or with an answer, or with both, and they would guaranty him a safe return. They then gave him his liberty. For a long time nothing was heard from the chief in reply to this message, nor from the captive English. Finally, an Indian woman entered Plymouth, and informed them that Obtakiest had received the message, but that it came too late to save the lives of the Englisn; he expressed great regret on this account, as he would have sent them back if they had been living. She also said, that he desired reconciliation with the English, but that his men were too fearful to come to Plymouth to negotiate a treaty; and that Obtakiest himself was so apprehensive of a sudden attack of the English, that he had no certain dwelling-place, but changed his encampment daily to avoid discovery.

This sudden and successful attack of Standish struck such terror into the Indians, as completely to arrest the execution of their conspiracy. So panic-stricken were they, that they abandoned their own dwellings and fled hither and thither, in woods, swamps, and other unfrequented places, as if they thought the whole English colony were in close pursuit. By their exposures during these flights, they caught various diseases, of which many of them died, among whom were Canacum, Aspinet and Ianough, the sachems of Buzzard's Bay, Eastham, and Barnstable. They had not courage even to plant their usual amount of corn, on which they were greatly dependent for food. At last the natives of one place ventured to man a small boat, and load it with presents, as a kind of peace-offering to the governor. On its voyage to the colony it was wrecked, and three of the men were lost. The only one who escaped did not dare to proceed to Plymouth, but returned. It is not unl kely that this catastrophe was interpreted by the Indians as unfavorable to themselves; for Ianough had given out that the God of the English was angry with the Indians, and was determined to destroy them. It would have been, therefore, very natural for them, under the influence of their superstitious fears, to have construed this disaster into an illustration of the truth of Ianough's prediction.

The Puritans kept their friends in England informed as fully as they could of the history of the colony. The conspiracy and its suppression, being important events, had a prominent place in their correspondence. When Mr. Robinson, their pastor at Leyden, who had commended them to God in earnest prayer, at the time of their departure from Delf Haven, heard of the slaughter of the Indians, his benevolent heart was painfully affected. He wrote a letter to the church at Plymouth, in which he exhorted them to consider the disposition of their captain, who was of a warm temper. "He hoped that the Lord had sent him among them for good, if they used him right," but at the same time expressed the fear that he may be wanting "in that tenderness of the life of man, made after God's image, which was meet." The overflowing benevolence of his soul burst forth in that memorable passage: "O, how happy a thing had it been, that you had converted some before you killed any!"

CHAPTER XI.

"With humble prayer and fasting,
  In every strait and grief,
They sought the Everlasting,
  And found a sure relief.
Their covenant-God o'ershadowed them,
  Their shield from every foe,
And gave them here a dwelling-place
  Two hundred years ago." — Rev. Dr. Flint.

The Conspiracy checked. — Arrival of a Blacksmith in disguise. — Who he is. — He hears unwelcome News. — He sails for Weymouth. — Is cast away and robbed. — Kindness of the Puritans. — Repaid with Ingratitude. — The Puritans without a Charter. — The Advantage of it. — Their first Patent. — The Ambition of John Pierce. — Is disappointed. — Arrival of more Immigrants and Stores. — The Distress of the Colony. — Admiral West. — Cannot subdue the Fishermen. — Community of Goods abandoned. — Self-Dependence. — Its Results. — The five Kernels of Corn. — No Bread! — Patience of the Sufferers. — Long Drought. — Day of Fasting and Prayer. — Refreshing Showers. — Effect upon the Natives.

So successful were the measures of Standish at Weymouth in intimidating the Indians, that no other attempt was made against the Plymouth colony for half a century. During this long period of quiet, the little settlement at Plymouth attained to some degree of maturity.

A short time after the return of Standish, and the abandonment of the plantation at Weymouth, a fishing vessel entered the harbor of Plymouth. A boat put off to the shore, bringing an Englishman, who pretended to be a blacksmith. He went among the colonists, inquiring about work, but at the same time asking many questions respecting the history and prospects of Weston's colony. He was informed of the conspiracy, of the massacre, and of the total abandonment of the place. This stranger was Weston himself in disguise! The intelligence he received fell upon his ear like the death-knell of his high hopes. The experiment of that plantation having involved a heavy expenditure, he was anxious to see if something had not been gained. At any rate, he wished to know the worst. He therefore took a shallop with two or three men, and set out to visit it. A heavy storm arose, which drove him from his course towards the Merrimac, where he was wrecked, and with difficulty escaped with his life. To complete his misfortunes, he was soon discovered by the Indians, who robbed him of all he had saved from the shallop, and stripped him of his clothes, even to his shirt. In this distressed condition he managed to reach Portsmouth, where he borrowed some clothes, returned to Plymouth, and entreated the Puritans to loan him some beaver. Although the colony was reduced to great straits, yet, in view of his greater wretchedness, it was concluded to lend him a hundred and seventy pounds of beaver. In this transaction the Puritans exhibited great kindness.

They were under no obligations to Weston. He had conferred upon them no favors. Though he was formerly interested in the Plymouth settlement, yet from personal considerations he abandoned it, and commenced one on his own account. The bad conduct of his settlers were, in all probability, the occasion of the Indian conspiracy and the massacre. They were extremely undesirable neighbors. Although they received nothing but good from the Puritans, in return they ridiculed and slandered them. Weston, therefore, had no claims upon Plymouth. The conduct of the Puritans in loaning him this beaver was unmerited kindness. This will be the more apparent, when it is remembered that he could give them no security.

With this borrowed capital Weston commenced his fortunes anew; yet such was his dishonesty and ingratitude, that he not only failed to pay for the beaver, but, instead thereof, he maligned and opposed the Puritans on every occasion. We cannot deem it any other than a fortunate circumstance, that his colony was broken up so early. With such a man at its head, and such characters for its materials as his colonists were, nothing could have been expected from its continuance but a series of internal dissensions among themselves, and of external troubles with the Indians.

When the Puritans left England in 1620, they

sailed under the protection of the Virginia company, with the intention of settling in Virginia, somewhere in the vicinity of Hudson's River. At that time, the territory of Virginia extended to the forty-fifth degree of north latitude, to Passamaquoddy Bay; but their patent having been taken out in the name of an individual, Mr. John Wincob, who did not accompany them, never rendered them any service. This appears like a misfortune; but, in reality, it was a blessing. Even if they could have made use of their patent, it was not what they wanted. It was essentially defective, inasmuch as it did not grant them what they desired above all things else — liberty of conscience; so that when they landed at Plymouth, they were unchartered, unpatented. They were in the wilderness, unfettered by any royal limits or "company" restrictions. Contrary to the design of the Virginia company, yea, contrary to their own intentions, they found themselves in a new world, three thousand miles from home, in the full enjoyment of liberty of conscience. God, in his kind providence, had given them that which the king, in his bigotry, would have withheld. In answer to their prayers, yet contrary to their hopes, the storms of Heaven had driven them into a harbor of freedom.

The first patent taken out for Plymouth was in the name of John Pierce, as trustee. This gentleman, seeing the prospective growth of the colony, had his ambition and covetousness so greatly excited, that he procured another patent for his own use, by means of which he intended to have held the colonists as his tenants, and to have compelled them "to sue in his courts as chief lord." But Providence was against him. He made two attempts to reach this country, from England, with a company of emigrants, and both times was driven back by disastrous storms. Being thwarted in his project by heavy losses, and other misfortunes, he was glad to sell to the Puritans, for five hundred pounds, his patent which had cost him but fifty.

The emigrants who had been driven back with Pierce came over in another vessel, called the Ann. She was soon followed by the Little James, who brought sixty passengers, and a quantity of supplies for the colony. These stores were very acceptable, as those of the Puritans were nearly gone. To so low a condition were they brought, that they had nothing better to extend to their newly arrived guests than lobsters and cold water. The importance of these stores may be inferred from the fact that a day was set apart for special thanksgiving and praise on account of this arrival.

In the month of June, 1623, one of the vessels in which Pierce had made one of his unsuccessful attempts to cross the Atlantic, arrived at Plymouth.

She was commanded by Captain Francis West, who had received the appointment of Admiral of New England, and had been commissioned to prevent all vessels from trading or fishing on the coast, without a license from the New England Council. But the fishermen being too independent and strong for him, he could not execute his commission. He gave it up as a hopeless undertaking, and sailed for Southern Virginia. To prevent any similar annoyance in future, the fishermen presented a petition to Parliament, who passed an order that fishing should be free.

Until this time, there had been a community of interest among the colonists. Each man raised what he chose, and threw it into a common stock, from which the overseers supplied to each family, according to their number. Land was not owned by individuals. It was all common. Each man cultivated what he pleased, and gave the products to the general store. This experiment of a community of goods, like many others which have been tried since, did not work well. As no wages could be given to any one for their labors in the field, and as those who were disposed to be idle were sure of their proportion of supplies, whether they worked or not, it was decided to abandon the system, and make every family support themselves. Accordingly, at a general meeting held in April of this year, (1623,) a certain portion of land was assigned to every man, by lot, for cultivation. All were, therefore, thrown upon their own labors for the fruits of the earth. Exceptions were made only in the case of public officers and of fishermen, who, being engaged for the welfare of the colony in other directions, were considered worthy of a share of the products of the soil, though they assisted not in raising them. Immediately after the allotment of the land, the men began to cultivate; yea, so great was the interest which had been excited by the new system, that women and children entered the fields, and labored so effectively, that a much larger quantity of corn was planted than was expected. This being over, they were again reduced to want. Their provisions were entirely consumed. A simple, affecting, yet very appropriate memorial of their condition at that time, was presented at the centennial celebration of their landing, which was observed December 22, 1820, at Plymouth. After an address from Hon. Daniel Webster, which occupied two hours in its delivery, and which was "correct in its historical statements, powerful in argument, rich in description, and pathetic and eloquent in action," a procession was formed, which marched to the new court-house, escorted by the STANDISH GUARDS, under the command of CAPTAIN WESTON. As they entered, to the sound of spirit-stirring music, the elegantly decorated hall, and passed down the long rows of tables, richly ladened with the luxuries of the sea and land, five kernels of parched corn were observed upon every plate. They attracted attention. Some smiled as they pâssed along, at what they regarded as an odd conceit. Others, who were better acquainted with the Yankee character, and with their fondness for significant notions, knew that these silent symbols were eloquent with some hidden meaning, whilst others, still, who perceived in a moment their design and their beautiful appropriateness to the occasion, gazed at them with a throbbing heart, and with tearful eyes. These five, mysterious kernels of corn were memorials of that affecting incident, when, in 1623, the colony were reduced to a pint of corn, which, when divided among the settlers, gave them five grains each! When this was understood at the table, it produced thrilling emotions. Those five grains of corn on each plate were full of the *farina* of thought and feeling. Some ate them with greater interest than the most costly luxuries before them; others carefully carried them away as mementoes of that occasion, and of the important event which was commemorated. It would not be surprising if some of those identical kernels are still sacredly treasured in the families of some who were present on that occasion. (See plate, p. 140.)

This tradition of the five kernels of corn, though it exhibits an affecting state of things, does not convey the worst of their condition. When these were gone, they had *no corn!* Other grain being out of the question, they of course had no bread! They were obliged to depend upon fish, clams, and oysters; occasionally, they would get a deer, which would be divided among the colony. In this manner was their good Elder Brewster supported for months together; yet he and his family, instead of repining at their hard lot, would sit down to their monotonous fare, giving thanks that they could "suck of the abundance of the seas, and of the treasures hid in the sand." This, we have reason to believe, was the disposition of the settlers generally; for Bradford, who was governor at that period, says, "By the time our corn is planted, our victuals are spent, not knowing at night where to have a bit in the morning, and have neither bread nor corn for THREE OR FOUR MONTHS TOGETHER, yet bear our wants with cheerfulness, and rest on Providence."

The unusually large quantity of corn which was planted, awakened hopes that in the following season they would have an abundant supply. But their hopes appeared doomed to be blasted. The cisterns in the skies were sealed up; the clouds withheld rain. The sun poured down its rays in the fulness of its strength. The earth turned to clods and dust. The leaves of the trees curled and withered. The grass was burnt up. Springs were exhausted, and brooks and ponds dried. For the long period of six weeks did the heavens withhold their showers. Their corn came up, but soon wilted; both blade and stalk hung down, changed color, and apparently died. Their beans "stood at a stay," dried up, turned yellow, and presented the appearance of having been scorched. Their hopes were overthrown; their joy turned to sorrow. Painful forebodings for the future filled their hearts. As an additional ingredient in their cup of woe, they heard that, many months before, supplies had been sent them from England; but the vessel which was bringing them was twice driven back, and was finally heard from, three hundred leagues at sea. As that intelligence was received three months before, as the vessel had not arrived, and as pieces of a wreck were found upon the coast, which they concluded were hers, they gave her up as lost. Their present and prospective trials were so great, that some began to be discouraged. They regarded these afflictions as indications of the displeasure of God against them. They were led to personal self-examination and prayer. In addition to these private religious exercises, a day of public humiliation, fasting, and prayer was appointed by the government. It was universally observed. The people assembled together with one accord. They abstained from food, confessed their sins, and offered fervent prayers, that if it were consistent with the will and the glory of God, he would send down upon them the rain and the dews of heaven, to refresh the thirsty earth, and revive the withering, dying plants. The day was kept with marked solemnity and earnestness. Their religious exercises continued through eight or nine hours. In the morning, the sky was as cloudless and unpromising, and the drought as likely to continue, as ever; but before the close of the meeting, "the weather," says Winslow in his relation, "was overcast, the clouds gathered together on all sides, and on the next morning, distilled such soft, sweet, and moderate showers of rain, continuing some fourteen days, and mixed with such seasonable weather, as it was hard to say whether our withered corn or drooping affections were most quickened or revived; such was the bounty and goodness of our God."

Hobbamock, who was *then at Plymouth,* seeing the people on their way to meeting, said it was but three days since Sunday. He wanted to understand the matter; he therefore asked a boy who was near him, "What are the people going to meeting for?" "To pray that God would give us rain." Hobbamock then informed the Indians that the Puritans were assembled together to worship their God, and pray to him to send down rain. No doubt those untaught, yet thoughtful savages watched with some degree of curiosity the result. When, therefore, they saw the clouds darken the heavens, and pour down such gentle, yet abundant showers, they admired the goodness which produced such delightful changes in so short a time. They were convinced that the English were under the protection of a great and good Being, who heard their prayers, and granted their requests.

The Five Kernels of Corn.

CHAPTER XII.

> "I, under fair pretence of friendly ends,
> And well-placed words of glossy courtesy,
> Baited with reason not unplausible,
> Wind me into the easy-hearted man,
> And hug him into snares." — MILTON.

John Lyford. — His Obsequiousness. — His Connection with John Oldham. — Governor Bradford takes Copies of their Letters. — Oldham rebels. — Lyford sets up a Meeting. — Their Trial. — The Governor's Address. — Both found guilty. — Oldham banished. — Lyford's Confession and deep Sorrow. — Repeats his Offence. — Oldham returns. — His abusive Conduct. — Sentenced to run the Gantlet. — He reforms. — Is killed by the Indians. — Timely Abundance. — Trade with the Kennebec. — A Return Ship captured. — Escape of Standish from Slavery. — Death of John Robinson. — His Character. — Death of Robert Cushman. — He preached the first Sermon in New England. — Its Character. — Extracts.

THE merchant adventurers in England, who had furnished the Puritans pecuniary assistance in their expedition to America, did not find it a very profitable speculation. Some of them were dissatisfied, and were ready to believe all the calumnies which the enemies of the colonists brought against them. There were not wanting men to originate the most false and libellous charges. Among these none were more prominent than John Lyford, an Episcopalian clergyman. He came over with Winslow, who had been sent to England as an agent of the colony. Upon his first arrival, Lyford hypocritically pretended to be a strong friend of the Puritans. He treated them with great reverence, "bowing and cringing" to them in a very obsequious manner, so much so that Governor Bradford was duped by him, and even invited him to his councils, in connection with Elder Brewster and others. He expressed a desire to be admitted to their church. After professing his belief in their doctrines and a reformation from all his sinful habits, he was received. It was not long before he contracted an intimacy with John Oldham, a man of turbulent and factious spirit, with whom he fomented discontents among the people. He was known to be very busy in preparing letters to send to England, when the vessel which brought him over should return. He, very foolishly for himself, made known the purport of his letters, and it was boasted among his friends that they would effect a complete overturn in the colony. The governor, fearing that the influence of his letters would be injurious to the interests of the colony, deemed it his duty to intercept them. After the vessel had set sail, he followed her in a small boat, and succeeded in overtaking her. He went on board and informed the captain of what he knew and what he feared. The captain, being a friend of the colony, permitted him to open the letters, both of Lyford and Oldham.

They were found to be filled with misrepresentations and malicious slanders against the church and the government. The design of the authors evidently was to procure the establishment of a new order of things, by means of which they hoped to ride into power. If these letters had been believed and heeded in England, the effects upon the colony would probably have been disastrous. The governor copied some, and kept the originals of others of these letters, sending copies of these latter to England. Some of this correspondence contained extracts from letters to the Puritans, which extracts Lyford obtained by unsealing the letters and taking copies when they were on board the vessel at Gravesend, England. This was done to increase the prejudice against them at home. When the governor returned, he made no disclosure of the discovery, but kept a more vigilant eye upon the two spies. The rogues, under the impression that their letters were on their way, unmolested, to England, and would react in their favor, became daily more emboldened, until Oldham rebelled against the constituted authorities, and stubbornly refused to take his regular turn in performing military duty and standing guard. Not satisfied with this, he rose against the captain with a deadly weapon, and violently opposed all who attempted to quiet him. He was tried, convicted, and sentenced to imprisonment. Upon his confession and promise of amendment, he was released.

Lyford developed his opposition in a more professional way. Without consultation with the governor, and without obtaining permission from either the church or the elder, he had the audacity to commence a meeting of his own on Lord's day, and with a few of his coadjutors to attempt the administration of the sacrament, by virtue of his episcopal ordination. This the Puritans could not permit. In the judgment of the governor, the time had now arrived when justice to the criminals, as well as the interests of the colony, demanded an open trial, with the exposure of their libellous correspondence. Accordingly, he called the whole colony together, and presented his complaints against the two offenders. They boldly denied the truth of the charges, and called for proof. Bradford now arose and gave an address of considerable length.

He stated that, as the Puritans were greatly oppressed and persecuted for their religious opinions in their own country, they had come to this land, that here they might enjoy their own views of truth and duty without molestation. He enlarged upon the painful labors and sufferings which this emigration had involved. He addressed Lyford, reminding him that though he had not shared in the early trials and expenditures of the colonists, yet when he and his family came over, they were received by the Puritans with great kindness, and freely supported, though it involved great expense; and now for him to plot the ruin of the colony, was an act of great "perfidy and ingratitude." Lyford persisted in his denial, and with great hypocrisy expressed astonishment at the charges, and said he did not understand the language which had been addressed to him. The governor now "put in" the letters as evidence. Lyford was confounded: Oldham was enraged, and added to the evidence against himself by calling upon his accomplices to be courageous, and take an open stand in the rebellion, and he would sustain them. But no one dared to show themselves upon his side. All feared the consequences, and kept aloof. The governor now continued his address to Lyford. He reminded him of his treachery in breaking the seals of private letters, and surreptitiously taking copies; of his humble confession when received into the church; of his promise not to perform the functions of a minister until he had another call to the sacred office, and yet, in open violation of this promise, he had assumed the clerical profession, drawn aside a small clique, and had attempted to officiate at the Lord's table!

Lyford's only defence was, that many persons in the colony had complained to him of various abuses which were practised. He gave their names: they were called upon to testify; but in so doing, they denied his assertions. With overwhelming evidence against him, and his own witnesses proving him a liar, he saw there was no hope of an acquittal. He burst into a flood of tears, confessed that his letters against them were false and malicious; said that he was a reprobate, and feared that his sins were too great to be forgiven. Both of them were found guilty, and sentenced to be expelled from the colony. Oldham was sent off at once. He was a pestilent fellow, and it was a great relief to the settlers to be freed from him. His wife and family were permitted to remain until they could be comfortably removed. The execution of Lyford's sentence was postponed for six months. It was the governor's intention to pardon him, in case his repentance proved sincere. Lyford made the most of this respite. His confessions were full and apparently penitent. He acknowledged that in his slanderous charges against the church and the government, he was influenced by unholy pride, ambition, and selfishness; and so great was his vileness, that if God should send him forth as a vagabond and fugitive upon the earth, it would be no more than he deserved. Such apparently sincere and hearty repentance could not be overlooked. Some were so solicitous in his behalf, that they were willing to intercede for his pardon on their knees. It seemed too cruel to exile such a tearful penitent.

Yet before one half of the time of his respite had elapsed, he was detected in a repetition of the offence. He actually wrote another libellous communication to his accomplices in England; but the bearer of it delivered it to the governor. Lyford now left the colony, and went to Cape Ann, where he had been invited as a minister. He afterwards died in Virginia.

When Oldham left Plymouth, he went to Nantasket. Notwithstanding his sentence prohibited his return without the permit of the governor, he came back the next march, at the time of the annual election. His conduct was so abusive and lawless, that his old acquaintances would not associate with him. He was arrested a second time, and sentenced to undergo the humiliating punishment of the gantlet. Two rows of armed soldiers were drawn up, and he was compelled to pass down the lines between them: as he passed each man gave him a blow with the but of his musket, and at the same time said, "Go and mend your manners." After this, Oldham became a trader at Nantasket. On a voyage to Virginia he was overtaken by a storm, and being in great peril, was frightened; made confession of his evil deeds, and promised God, that if his life were preserved, he would mend his ways. After this he so far reformed that the colonists at Plymouth permitted him to visit them whenever he chose. He was finally killed in a quarrel with some Indians.

The company of merchant adventurers who had assisted the Puritans, being disappointed in their expectations of profit, and involved in pecuniary embarrassments, dissolved, and threw the colonists to a greater extent than ever upon themselves. This was in 1625. A kind Providence so ordered it that, just at the time when they were abandoned by the adventurers at home, their crops proved unusually abundant. They not only had corn enough for their own use, but a surplus for traffic. They desired to send some of it to Kennebec. But how could they get it there? They had no horses or other beasts of burden, and, therefore, could not take it by land. All their shipping amounted to only two small shallops, which, in their present condition, would not answer the purpose. After some consultation they built a deck over one of the shallops, and loaded it with corn. As there were no sailors in the colony, the shallop was manned by Mr. Winslow and some of the most experienced men. They set out upon this "commercial" enterprise late in the fall. It proved successful. They made a profitable exchange with their corn, and brought back seven hundred pounds of beaver, besides other peltries. Not the least advantage gained on that occasion was the finding of a market for future trade.

The same year Capt. Standish had a narrow escape from slavery. Two ships, which had come from the adventurers on a trading voyage, were about to return with a cargo of fish and furs. It being necessary that Standish should go to London as agent for the colony, he embarked in one of these vessels. The larger ship took the smaller one in tow, until they arrived at the English channel. Here it was cast off, and before it could reach London it was overtaken by a Turkish man-of-war, captured, and taken to Salee, in the kingdom of Fez, where the captain and crew were reduced to slavery. If Standish had been on board, that would have been his fate; but, fortunately, he was in the larger vessel, and so escaped. When he returned to Plymouth the next year, he brought back the intelligence of the death of their pastor, the venerable and beloved John Robinson. This was a painful blow to the colony. Robinson had been their pastor for many years. When persecution raged too violently for them in their own country, where they were subjected to imprisonments and other penalties on account of their religious views, he fled with them to Leyden, in Holland, and shared in their trials whilst residents among a people whose language they understood not, and where they found great difficulty in obtaining a support. When their emigration to America was resolved on, Robinson heartily favored it. Lest any might waver in the determination which they had formed, he preached a sermon to encourage in them a firmness of purpose to remove. At a later period in the same year, a day of special fasting and prayer was appointed, when he preached to them again from that very apposite passage recorded in Ezra viii. 21: "I proclaimed a fast at the river Ahava, that we might afflict ourselves before God, to seek of him a right way for us, and for our little ones, and for all our substance." The sermon was fraught with judicious and timely advice. It breathed a spirit of Christian liberality which contrasted widely with the prevailing bigotry of the times. It expressed the conviction that even they had not arrived at a discovery of the whole mind of God, as revealed in the Scriptures, and, therefore, they ought to expect the unfolding of new truths, which he exhorted them to be ever ready to receive. He cautioned them against following him any farther than his conduct was in accordance with the example of the Savior. "Brethren," said he, "we are now quickly to part from one another, and whether I may ever live to see your face on earth any more, the God of heaven only knows; but whether the Lord hath appointed that or not, I charge you before God and his blessed angels, that you follow me no farther than you have seen me follow the Lord Jesus Christ. If God reveal any thing to you, by any other instrument of his, be as ready to receive it as ever you were to receive any truth by my ministry: for I am fully persuaded, I am very confident, that the Lord has more truth yet to break forth out of his holy word. For my part, I cannot sufficiently bewail the condition of the reformed churches, who are come to a period in religion, and will go at present no farther than the instruments of their reformation. The Lutherans cannot be drawn to go beyond what Luther saw. Whatever part of his will our good God has revealed to Calvin, they will rather die than embrace it; and the Calvinists, you see, stick fast where they were left by that great man of God, who yet saw not all things." Robinson was a man of "good genius, quick penetration, ready wit, great modesty, integrity, and candor." With a good classical education, strong powers of argument, and an aptness to detect and expose the weak points of his opponents, he was acknowledged to be a formidable disputant. In his personal intercourse he was easy, gentlemanly, and obliging. As a preacher, he was impressive and edifying. He increased in blandness of manners as he advanced in years. He was particularly distinguished as a peacemaker, and was the means, in a number of instances, of effecting a reconciliation between those who were at variance with each other. His death was greatly lamented by both branches of the church.

In addition to the decease of Robinson, Captain Standish also brought intelligence of the death of Mr. Robert Cushman, a gentleman who had been deeply interested in the welfare of the colony from the first. He embarked, as has already been stated, with the first company that left England for Plymouth; but when the Speedwell was abandoned, and all could not be accommodated in the Mayflower, he was among the number who were left behind. He came out afterwards in the Fortune. It is a singular circumstance that he, being a layman, preached the first sermon ever delivered in New England. It was on the "Sin and Danger of Self-love," from the text, "Let no man seek his own, but every man another's wealth." It was printed in London, anonymously, in 1622, and has passed through several editions in this country. Tradition has fixed the spot where it was delivered, at the house of the plantation, on the south side of Leyden Street. The plan of the sermon was as follows: "The parts of this text are two. 1. A dehortation. 2. An exhortation. The dehortation: Let no man seek his own. The exhortation: But every man another's wealth. In handling of which, I will first open the words; secondly, gather the doctrine; thirdly, illustrate the doctrine by Scriptures, experience, and reason; fourthly, apply the same to every one his portion." It was a discourse of marked peculiarities, abounding with good thoughts, quaintly expressed, according to the fashion of the times. We give one extract as a specimen. "The difference between a temperate, good man and a belly-god is this: A good man will not eat his morsels alone, especially if he have better than others; but if by God's providence he have gotten some meat which is better than ordinary, and better than his other brethren, he can have no rest in himself, except he make others partake with him. But a belly-god will slop all in his own throat, yea, though his neighbor come in and behold him eat; yet this gripple-gut shameth not to swallow all." He was sent twice to England, as agent of the colony, and managed their business with great discretion.

CHAPTER XIII.

> "I venerate the man whose heart is warm,
> Whose hands are pure, whose doctrine and whose life,
> Coincident, exhibit lucid proof
> That he is honest in the sacred cause." — COWPER.

A Pinnace built. — Messengers from the Dutch. — Reception of De Razier. — Trade with him. — Wampum. — The Colony without a Pastor. — Original Agreement respecting their old Pastor. — A Minister found at Nantasket. — He becomes the Plymouth Pastor. — His Character. — Roger Williams. — His Troubles at Salem. — Goes to Plymouth as an Assistant. — Returns to Salem. — He cultivates Acquaintance with the Natives. — John Billington. — Commits Murder. — Is tried and executed. — The Tendency of Sin. — A Shipwreck. — Kindness of the Indians. — Difficulties adjusted. — Governor Winthrop's Visit to Plymouth. — Singular Puritan Custom. — Discussion about the Use of "Goodman Such-a-one." — Hue's Cross.

IN order to carry on a trade with their southern neighbors, the colonists, in 1627, built a small pinnace at Buzzard's Bay. By transporting their merchandise overland from Plymouth to that point, a distance of only a few miles, they avoided a comparatively long and dangerous voyage round Cape Cod. They accomplished, in this manner, two objects; they escaped danger, and saved time. A similar method of conveyance was resorted to in 1812, at the time of our last war with Great Britain, in order to escape the enemy who were cruising about the Cape.

In 1627, letters and messengers from the Dutch settlements on the Hudson River arrived at Plymouth, conveying friendly congratulations, and proposing commercial intercourse. They were cordially received, and their sentiments of friendship met with a hearty response. In September of the same year, Isaac De Razier, who had signed the above letters as secretary, came himself to Buzzard's Bay. From thence, he sent a request to Governor Bradford for a boat to bring him to Plymouth. The boat was soon got in order and sent, and the honorable secretary was brought to Plymouth, with the music of trumpeters, in genuine Dutch style. His arrival was quite an exciting event in the little town, and furnished the Puritans with new topics of conversation. He and his company were hospitably entertained for several days. When he returned, a number of the colony accompanied him as far as Buzzard's Bay. As he had brought with him sugar, linen, and other articles which they needed, they made a number of purchases, which were mutually advantageous, and then, with reciprocal expressions of respect, they parted. The way being once opened, the Dutch frequently visited Buzzard's Bay, and exchanged their productions for those of Plymouth. Among the articles which they obtained from the Dutch was a quantity of wampum, or wampum-peack; or, as Gookin calls it, wompompague. It is composed of small pieces of shell, white or purple, ground, polished, and then drilled, so that they may be strung. They were used by the Indians as coin. The first quantity which the Puritans bought they found very difficult to dispose of. They kept it on hand for two years. After this it became a very salable article, especially among the Indians of the interior, with whom fragments of sea-shell were rare. One fathom of it was equivalent to five shillings. They sent large quantities of it to Kennebec, where, by their monopoly of it, they succeeded in obtaining command of the whole trade on that river.

When the Puritans first came over in the Mayflower, they were unaccompanied by any pastor.

It had been previously agreed upon by the Leyden church, that if the majority came over with the first party, they should be accompanied by their pastor, but if only a minority of the church came, Elder Brewster should be their religious teacher, and the pastor should tarry with the majority. This arrangement was faithfully executed. As only a minority came with the first company, Robinson was left behind to take charge of the others, but Brewster accompanied the emigrants; hence, after their arrival, public religious services were usually conducted by him. He was a man well qualified to have become their pastor, but resolutely refused ordination.

After the death of Robinson, that branch of the church over which he had presided was dissolved, and a portion of them, among whom were his widow and children, came to Plymouth. Still, Brewster continued unwilling to be ordained, although he performed the regular duties of pastor. This state of things continued until 1629, when some of the men of Plymouth, having occasion to put into Nantasket, found there a man reduced to a destitute condition, by the name of Ralph Smith. He earnestly entreated them to take him to Plymouth. As he appeared to be an honest-hearted, ingenuous, and pious man, and had officiated as a minister, they complied with his request. After he had been at Plymouth a short time, and had exercised his gifts among them, he was invited to become their pastor. This invitation being accepted, he was settled over them as their first minister. They were not long in discovering that he was a man of limited intelligence and weak capacity. There was a wide disparity between his instructions and those of their revered Robinson. The teachings of Brewster were regarded as far more edifying than his. It was no easy task to fill the places of such men. This Smith himself painfully realized. He felt his inability to meet the wants of his flock, and, after occupying his position five or six years, he finally, under a personal sense of his incapacity, and in compliance with the request

14

of his people, tendered his resignation. Before he left, he was assisted in his labors by the renowned Roger Williams, who came over on the 5th of February, 1630. Mr. Williams first accepted of the invitation of the church in Salem to settle with their pastor, Mr. Skelton, as an assistant teacher. But the civil government soon interfered and sent a letter to the church, censuring them for choosing Mr. Williams "without advising with the council," and desiring them to proceed no farther until they had a conference on the subject. Charges of an ecclesiastical or theological nature were brought against Mr. Williams by the secular authorities. He was condemned for his religious views by the General Court. His condition at Salem was made uncomfortable by "the powers that be," who ought to have let him alone. Though he and his church were mutually and strongly attached to each other, he thought it best to accept of the invitation to be an assistant teacher at Plymouth. His labors there were well received. Governor Bradford says of him, "He exercised his gifts among us, and after some time was admitted a member of the church, and his teaching was well approved; for the benefit whereof, I shall bless God, and am thankful to him even for his sharpest admonitions and reproofs, so far as they agreed with truth." And Morton asserts that "he was well accepted as an assistant in the ministry."

He remained about two years at Plymouth, during which time he probably expressed his sentiments upon those subjects which were so obnoxious to the government of Massachusetts, and which were not particularly agreeable to the leading men of Plymouth, though they were not condemned by any formal act of the church. His attachment to Salem was not destroyed. Being invited to return there as an assistant to Mr. Skelton, who was in declining health, he asked a dismission from the Plymouth church. His friends were unwilling to grant it. But Mr. Brewster, the ruling elder, advised the church to comply with his request, and dismiss both him and his adherents, which was accordingly done. He then went to Salem, accompanied by those who had become attached to his ministry. Mr. Williams was the great champion of soul-liberty. He maintained the principle of universal religious toleration, and contended that the civil government had no right to interfere with the religious belief of men; that "the civil power has no jurisdiction over the conscience." In these respects he was far ahead of his age. But what were regarded as novel and dangerous sentiments in his day, are now admitted truths, and familiar as household words.

During his residence at Plymouth, he availed himself of every favorable opportunity of intercourse with the Indians. He made excursions among them to learn their language, study their manners, and qualify himself to be useful among them. "My whole desire," said he, in one of his letters, "was to do the natives good." He became acquainted with the most influential chiefs, and secured their friendship by the interest which he manifested for their welfare. In a letter written near the evening of life, he says, "God was pleased to give me a painful, patient spirit, to lodge with them in their filthy, smoky holes, (even while I lived at Plymouth and Salem,) to gain their tongue." The knowledge which he thus acquired, and the friendships he formed, were of great service to him in after-life. But as the history of his subsequent adventures were not connected with Plymouth colony, it will not be appropriate to dwell upon them here.

During the first ten years of the settlement of the colony, no capital offence was committed. But at the end of that period, a murder was perpetrated, which required careful investigation. The culprit was John Billington, a profane, miserable scapegrace from London, who in some unaccountable manner was "shuffled" in among the pilgrims, and came over in the Mayflower. He was guilty of the first offence in the colony, an account of which has been already given, and for which he was sentenced to have his neck and heels tied together. Governor Bradford said of him, in a letter to Mr. Cushman in

1625, "Billington is a knave, and so will live and die." Whether this prediction was fulfilled or not, we shall see in the sequel. A complaint being entered against him, the case was first examined by a grand jury, and as they found a true bill, charging him with waylaying and killing a young man by the name of John Newcomen, he was tried by a petit jury, who, after a careful hearing of the evidence in the case, brought in a verdict of guilty. It became now a grave question with the government, What shall be done? Here is a murderer on our hands, who, after a fair trial according to the rules of law, has been found guilty. By the laws of England, he ought to die. But if we judge him according to English laws, by that act we shall acknowledge ourselves subject to English laws and under obligation to obey them, whereas we have fled to this wilderness to escape that necessity. Besides, have we authority to execute him? Or, in his execution shall we not incur the liability of a prosecution by the home government? It was regarded as a matter of such grave importance, and involving such difficult points, that it was resolved to ask the advice of the governor and some of the most judicious men of the neighboring colony of Massachusetts Bay. The facts in the case were accordingly communicated to them, and their opinions solicited. Governor Winthrop, and the others who had been consulted, were unanimous in the conclusion that the murderer ought to die. They based their opinion not upon English law, but upon the law of Moses, that whoso sheddeth man's blood, by man shall his blood be shed. They advised, therefore, that the criminal should be executed, and "the land be purged of blood." Their advice was followed, and poor John Billington suffered an ignominious death. He furnished another illustration of the progressiveness and fatal tendency of sin. If the punishment which he received for the first offence committed in the colony had been effectual in his reformation, he might have lived a useful life, and died an honored death. But no; notwithstanding his professed penitence on that occasion, and the favor which was shown him, he pressed on in his career of iniquity, until he came to an ignoble end. So true it is that evil men and seducers wax worse and worse, deceiving and being deceived; and that lust, when it hath conceived, bringeth forth sin; and sin, when it is finished, bringeth forth death.

It is refreshing to turn from the cruelty of Billington to the kindness of certain *savages* which was exhibited about the same time. Richard Garrett, with a number of others who belonged to the more recent settlement at Boston, was driven ashore at Cape Cod. Their vessel went to pieces. It being in the cold season, a number of the men perished from exposure and hardship. Others of them, though they did not die, suffered greatly, and had a very narrow escape. The Indians on the cape rallied to their rescue. Those of the survivors who were almost exhausted they attended and nursed with great kindness, until they were completely restored; the dead bodies of the others they buried, though with difficulty, in consequence of the ground being frozen; and then, taking those who were recovered, they escorted them for fifty miles through woods and fields, until they brought them safely to Plymouth.

The two neighboring colonies of Plymouth and Massachusetts Bay were on the verge of a quarrel, in consequence of the trade in corn, which the latter carried on with the Indians at Cape Cod. A pinnace which belonged to Salem was driven by stress of weather into Plymouth. She was found to be laden with corn. The colonists were anxious to know where it was obtained. When they learned that it had been purchased of the natives at Cape Cod, they were displeased, and the governor issued an order forbidding the traffic, and threatening that the order should be forcibly executed if any attempt was made to continue the trade. This led to a correspondence between the governors of the two colonies, and after a visit from Governor Bradford to Boston, the difficulty was adjusted.

Next year, 1632, Governor Winthrop, of Massachusetts, made a visit to Plymouth, accompanied by his pastor, Rev. Mr. Wilson, and two captains. They embarked in a vessel commanded by Captain Pierce, which had recently arrived from England, and were put on shore at Weymouth, where another colony had been planted after the destruction of Weston's, and which had met with some degree of prosperity. On the next morning they started for Plymouth, which they reached at evening of the same day. They were honorably received, hospitably entertained and "feasted every day at several houses." The Sabbath being communion day, they partook of the ordinance of the supper. Winthrop in his journal has given a particular account of certain forms which were observed on that occasion. He says, "In the afternoon Mr. Roger Williams (according to their custom) propounded a question, to which their pastor, Mr. Smith, spake briefly. Rev. Mr. Williams prophesied; and after, the governor of Plymouth spake to the question; after him, the elder; then some two or three more of the congregation. Then the elder desired the governor of Massachusetts and Mr. Wilson to speak to it, which they did. When this was ended, the deacon, Mr. Fuller, put the congregation in mind of the contribution, upon which the governor and all the rest *went down to the deacon's seat and put into the bag*, and then returned." From this it would seem that the contribution box or bag was not passed round; but every one who contributed, the governors with the rest, left his place, went down to the deacon's seat, which was probably near, or under, the pulpit, and there left their offering. On the following Wednesday, the Massachusetts governor, with his suite, left for home. They were accompanied part of their way by the governor, the pastor, and the elder of Plymouth.

This is not the whole of this interesting visit which has come down to us. Cotton Mather, in his Magnalia, has given a characteristic account of the question which was discussed, and some of the arguments employed on that occasion. It sheds additional light upon the spirit and temper of those times. He states that "there were at this time, in Plymouth, two ministers leavened so far with the humors of the rigid separation, that they insisted vehemently upon the unlawfulness of calling any unregenerate man by the name of *Goodman Such-a-one*, until, by their indiscreet urging of this whimsey, the place began to be disquieted. The wiser people being troubled at these trifles, they took the opportunity of Governor Winthrop's being there, to have the thing publicly propounded in the congregation; who, in answer thereunto, distinguished between a theological and a moral goodness, adding, that when juries were first used in England, it was usual for the crier, after the names of persons fit for that service were called over, to bid them all *attend, good men and true;* whence it grew to be a civil custom in the English nation for neighbors, living by one another, to call one another Goodman Such-a-one, and it was pity now to make a stir about a civil custom so innocently introduced. And that speech of Mr. Winthrop put a lasting stop to the little, idle, whimsical conceits then beginning to grow obstreperous."

On their return home, they came to a place named Hue's Cross. The religious antipathies of the governor were excited, and for fear that, at some subsequent period, the papists might assert that this name was evidence of their religion being first known in this country, he ordered it to be called Hue's Folly. Thus, in a peculiar sense, did the cross become foolishness.

CHAPTER XIV.

"In such a time as this, it is not meet
That every nice offence should bear its comment." — SHAKSPEARE.

Sir Christopher Gardner. — Foments Trouble. — Is charged with Bigamy. — Is pursued. — Is delivered up by Indians. — Indian Custom to secure a Welcome. — Small-pox. — Trade extended. — Adventures on the Connecticut. — Troubles on the Kennebec. — Captain Hocking killed. — A Plymouth Magistrate arrested in Boston. — Excitement at Plymouth. — Deputies sent to Boston. — Prayer before Business. — The Defence. — The Confession. — The Adjustment. — A Hurricane. — Its dreadful Ravages. — Eclipse of the Moon.

THE next year, both of the colonies had trouble with the home government, in consequence of the charge of rebellion which was alleged against them by Sir Christopher Gardner, who, it is supposed, was stimulated to this perfidy by Sir Ferdinando Gorges and Captain Mason, whose aspirations were for a general government over the whole of New England. Sir Christopher was a man of some distinction. He was related to Gardner, the bishop of Winchester, and was, in heart, a papist. When he first arrived in Massachusetts, he professed a deadness to the things of this world, and expressed a desire for retirement, where he could give himself to the cultivation of personal piety, without molestation. He applied to several churches for admission to membership; but as he was attended by a handsome young woman, whom he passed off as his cousin, but to whom he was suspected of sustaining a criminal relation, his application was refused. It was reported that he had two wives in England. When this accusation reached the government of Massachusetts, they determined to arrest him. Being informed of their design, Gardner fled from their jurisdiction, and concealed himself among the Namasket Indians, within the limits of the Plymouth colony. These Indians revealed his place of seclusion to Governor Bradford, who authorized them to seize him and conduct him to Plymouth, but to inflict upon him no injury. After this, the natives were on the alert for their victim. They discovered him at a short distance from a river, and attempted to apprehend him. He fled from them, leaped into a canoe, and pushed off in the river. Being armed with a musket and rapier, he was able to keep his pursuers at a respectful distance, especially as they were ordered to do him no injury. If they had been commanded to bring him to the colony, dead or alive, by letting fly a shower of arrows upon him, they could easily have complied. As it was, they found it difficult to apprehend him without a violation of the prohibition. Soon, an accident occurred in their favor. As the fugitive was floating down the stream, his canoe dashed upon a rock, and was immediately overturned. His rapier and gun dropped in the water, and were lost. A small dagger was left, which he immediately drew. As the Indians were unwilling either to inflict or to receive injury, they did not approach him very closely. They pursued a different method. They obtained some long poles, and, whilst standing at a considerable distance, they rapped him on the knuckles, and knocked the dagger from his hands. Resistance was then unavailing, and he yielded. He was taken to Plymouth; from thence, at the requisition of Governor Winthrop, he was removed to Boston as a prisoner, and, soon after, sent back to England. The charge of rebellion which he preferred against the colonies was so amply rebutted, — so satisfactory was the defence of the colonists, — that King Charles said "he would have them severely punished, who did abuse his government and plantation." The defendants were dismissed with expressions of favor.

Governor Winthrop relates an incident as illustrative of a singular custom among the Indians. Mr. Winslow had been for some time absent on an excursion to the west, as far as Connecticut. On his return, he left his vessel at Narraganset, with the intention of journeying the rest of the way to Plymouth by land. Massasoit, his old friend and patient, offered to be his guide. But before they commenced their march, the chief sent a courier ahead, to tell the colonists that Winslow was dead, and to show them the spot where he was slain. When the courier reached Plymouth, and communicated the mournful intelligence, it produced deep and universal sorrow, as Winslow was one of their principal men, and greatly beloved. The next day, Massasoit arrived, bringing Winslow with him, alive and well. Then was there a sudden change in the feelings of the Puritans. Sorrow endured for a night; joy came in the morning. When Massasoit was examined as to the reason for sending this false messenger, he replied that it was one of the customs of his people, to render their return the more welcome after an absence from home.

In 1634, the small-pox extensively prevailed among the Indians. Large numbers were swept away.

For a few years past, the colony at Plymouth had been gradually extending their trade with the Indians, in various directions, as far as the Kennebec on the east, and the Connecticut on the west. As rival colonies had sprung up at different points, collisions sometimes took place between them, in respect to their rights of trade with certain tribes. Plymouth became involved in trouble with the Dutch of Manhattan, and with her nearer neighbor, the Massachusetts colony. To avoid minuteness of

SIR CHRISTOPHER GARDNER TAKEN.

detail in these affairs, we shall content ourselves with the narration of one or two incidents only.

A Plymouth vessel was lying in the Connecticut River, in close proximity to a Dutch fort. The merchant and most of the crew were on shore, unsuspicious of danger. A Captain Stone, a "West Indian of St. Christopher's," obtained an interview with the commander of the Dutch fort, and plied him so copiously with spirituous potations as to produce intoxication. He then obtained the Dutchman's leave to take the Puritan vessel which was lying in the river. He did so, and immediately fled with his prize towards Virginia. Some Dutch sailors who were under obligations to the Puritans for kindnesses which they had received from them at Plymouth, perceiving Stone's villanous purpose, and being determined to defeat it, if possible, pursued him in two vessels, overtook him, and recaptured the prize. Sometime after this, Stone was in Massachusetts, where the officers of the law served him with a process. To effect a compromise, he went to Plymouth. In a misunderstanding which he had with the governor, not being satisfied with using hard words, he drew a weapon, and would have plunged it into him, if he had not been restrained by the governor's attendants. After this, he returned to Connecticut. Being asleep in the cabin of his vessel, in company with a Captain

Norton, he was attacked by the savages. Norton exhibited great bravery in the struggle which followed. Some gunpowder which had been carelessly left upon a table, in the melee took fire. The explosion blinded Norton to such a degree that he could no longer defend himself. Both were slain. The pirates then plundered the vessel, fled, and concealed themselves among the Pequot tribe. This was among the causes that led to the Pequot war.

Not far from this time, two of the magistrates of Plymouth were on the Kennebec, at a point embraced within the limits of the Plymouth patent. Whilst there, a pinnace, owned by Lords Say and Seal, and under the command of Hocking, entered the Kennebec, and attempted to pass up, for the purpose of trafficking with the natives. The Plymouth magistrates forbade him. He refused to comply with their embargo. He insisted upon going up, and insolently told them he would ascend the river, trade with the Indians in defiance of them, and would "lie there as long as he pleased." As he persevered in his determination, the Plymouth men followed him in a boat, entreating him to return. He replied with insulting language and blunt denials. As words produced no effect, they resorted to other measures. When the pinnace came to anchor, they approached it in a canoe, and severed one of the cables, and attempted to treat the other in the same manner. Hocking declared that, if they did not desist, he would shoot them. They dared him to do it, and persevered in the use of their knives upon the remaining cable. He now fired, and one of them in the canoe fell dead! They returned the fire, and killed Hocking! This was an unfortunate affair: it was adapted to excite prejudices against the Puritans, and, as Governor Winthrop said at the time, "to bring them all and the gospel under a common reproach of cutting one another's throats for beaver." In May, Mr. John Alden, a magistrate of Plymouth, visited Boston. As he was present at the time of the above catastrophe, one of the relatives of Hocking made a complaint against him in General Court, and had him arrested and held to bail. Winthrop, governor of Massachusetts, then wrote to the colony of Plymouth, informing them of the arrest, and wishing to know whether they would see that justice was done, as the affair happened in their jurisdiction. He also informed them that they made the arrest as a public expression of their condemnation of the deed.

When this letter was received, and the Plymouth colony were informed that one of their magistrates was arrested and under bail in Boston, it produced no small degree of excitement. It was considered an affair of such grave importance, that ex-governors Bradford and Winslow, with Mr. Smith, their pastor, visited Boston, and met, in conference on the subject, the magistrates and ministers of the latter place, among whom were Governor Winthrop, Mr. Wilson, and Mr. Cotton. In this interview, we have another development of the devotional character of the Puritans, and of their dependence upon a higher power for guidance in times of perplexity; we see how they mingled prayer with their business conferences. It was not until after "they had sought the Lord," that they entered upon their deliberations. The Plymouth gentlemen contended that they had an exclusive right to the trade of the Kennebec; that Hocking was guilty of a trespass, and that, as he fired first, the one who killed him did it in self-defence. They still, however, acknowledged themselves under some degree of guilt, "in that they did hazard man's life for such a cause, and did not rather wait to preserve their rights by other means." They also promised to be more careful, and avoid similar offences in future. The result of this conference was so favorable, that Governors Winthrop and Dudley, of Massachusetts, used their influence in England in behalf of Plymouth. Lords Say and Seal, in whose employ Hocking was, at the time of his death, though at first they were highly enraged, upon learning the true facts in the case, "were pacified."

On the 15th of August, 1635, Plymouth was

visited by one of the most powerful hurricanes which has ever been experienced in this climate. It commenced just before daylight, and gradually increased, until its violence was most terrific. It converted the bay into an ocean of mountain billows ; vessels were swallowed up, or dashed to fragments upon the rock-bound coast. In some places the tide rose twenty feet perpendicularly, so that the affrighted Indians were obliged to ascend trees, and cling to the branches, to prevent themselves from being swept away. Many houses were laid level with the ground, and the roofs of many others were lifted, broken, and whirled through the air like leaves from the forest. All the corn which had been planted was prostrated to the earth, but being advanced far towards maturity, it was not absolutely destroyed. Morton says, "It blew down many hundred thousand of trees," breaking some short off; tearing up others by the roots, whilst the tall young oaks and walnuts it twisted and wound, like withes. It presented a wild and fearful scene, and left the marks of its ravages for many years. It came from the south-east, changed its direction frequently, and continued in its greatest violence six hours. Two nights afterward there was a great eclipse of the moon.

CHAPTER XV.

"Justice, like lightning, ever should appear
To few men's ruin, but to all men's fear." — SWETNAM.

"Justice must be from violence exempt;
But fraud 's her only object of contempt;
Fraud in the fox, force in the lion dwells,
But justice both from human hearts expels." — DENHAM.

An Indian murdered. — Four Englishmen in Want. — They visit Roger Williams. — Are found to be the Murderers. — Three are caught. — Their Trial. — Singular Difficulty. — They are executed. — Effect of Puritan Justice on the Indians. — Anecdote of Captain Standish. — Alden takes his new Bride home on a Bull. — Confederation of the New England Colonies. — Germ of the American Union. — Its Influence. — Indian Alliances. — The Removal of the whole Colony proposed. — The Subject considered by the Church. — Purchase Eastham. — Found to be more unfavorable than Plymouth. — The Project abandoned. — Ex-Governor Prince settles at Eastham.

AFTER the execution of Billington, the account of which we have already given, no murder was committed in the colony until 1638. This year an Indian, who had made a trade for the son of Canonicus, the chief, and was returning home, with three coats and five fathom of wampum, seated himself in the woods near the edge of a swamp, probably to rest. Whilst there, four Englishmen came along and spoke to him. One of them asked him to "drink tobacco" with them, (a phrase which they used for smoking.) He arose and went towards the individual who had so kindly given him the invitation, and, as he reached forth his hand to receive the offered pipe, this professed friend thrust a deadly weapon through his leg into his abdomen. The Indian sprang back, when the other made a second plunge, but failed to reach him. Then one of the others followed; but his blow missed, and his weapon stuck in the ground. The wounded Indian now fled. They pursued him, but he was successful in eluding them. After they had gone, the poor fellow crawled back with great pain, and laid himself in the path that he might be discovered and receive help. This transpired at Pawtucket, near Providence, but within the precincts of Plymouth colony.

Soon after this, an Indian passing through Providence, informed Roger Williams that there were four Englishmen at Pawtucket, about four miles distant, almost starved for want of food. With his characteristic kindness, Mr. Williams immediately sent them provisions, spirits, and a cordial invitation to visit Providence. When the messenger returned, he informed Mr. Williams that one of them was Arthur Peach, of Plymouth, an *Irishman*, and another was called John Barnes. They pleaded the fatigues and soreness of travelling, as their excuse for declining his invitation. The next morning, however, they came, stating that they were turned out of the house where they were at Pawtucket, because some Indians said they had wounded an *Englishman*. They pretended that they had lost their way in going from Plymouth to Weymouth, and afterwards in coming from Weymouth to Providence. The Sabbath which had elapsed since they left Plymouth, they said they spent in resting in the woods. Shortly after they had left Providence, an old Indian arrived there and informed Mr. Williams, that whilst four Englishmen were stopping at Pawtucket, three natives arrived, saying that they had found an Indian almost dead in the woods, who had been attacked by four Englishmen. They inquired whether there were any English there, or whether any had been seen. When Arthur and his companions heard of these inquiries, they got up and fled hastily in the night. So soon as Mr. Williams understood the facts in the case, he sent a messenger in pursuit of the English, whilst himself went to the wounded man in the woods and ministered, Samaritan-like, to his wants. Three of the Englishmen were apprehended at Rhode Island, and sent to Plymouth, where they were brought to trial. The court consisted of the wisest, most experienced, and best men of the colony, embracing Bradford, Winslow, Prince, Standish and others of similar character. A singular difficulty occurred at the trial, which, in some courts, might have resulted in the acquittal of the prisoners, and in others would have led to a postponement of the trial. Here were three men tried for murder, and none of the witnesses could swear that the wounded man was dead. Mr. Williams and a Mr. James of Providence testified that the wound inflicted was mortal, and two Indians in court swore that if he were not dead from the injury he received, they would be willing to die themselves. They were found guilty and executed. Before their execution they made a full confession of the crime, and acknowledged that they did it in order to obtain the Indian's wampum. The one who escaped concealed himself for a season, and afterwards left the country. In the execution of these three colonists for one Indian, the Puritans exhibited their strong sense of justice, and their firm determination to protect, not only themselves, but also the natives, in the possession of their just rights. It was important that the Indians should be convinced of this, as otherwise, when injuries were done them, they would take the law into their own hands and inflict summary punishment. This execution, which, so far as we know, was unsought for on their part, must have convinced them of the certainty of colonial protection. For many years they made no attempts to avenge the injuries they received from individual colonists, but left the execution of justice, in such cases, to the English.

It will be a relief to the above sombre proceedings, if we relate here the following traditionary anecdote of one of the above jurymen, which illustrates the danger of one gentleman commissioning another to make proposals of marriage for him to the lady whose hand he seeks.

A short time after the death of Mrs. Standish, the bereaved captain found his heart filled with tender interest for Miss Priscilla Mullins, daughter of Mr. William Mullins. He cherished the impression that if she could be persuaded to unite her fortunes with his, the loss which he had experienced would be repaired. He, therefore, according to Puritan custom, made known his wishes to the father through Mr. John Alden, as his messenger. Mullins made no objection, although he might reasonably have done so, on account of the decease of Mrs. Standish having been so recent. He gave his consent, but informed Alden that the young lady must be consulted. Priscilla was called into the room, not knowing for what purpose she was wanted. Alden, a man of noble form, of fair, and somewhat florid complexion, and engaging manners, arose and delivered his message for Standish in befitting language, and in a prepossessing, courteous style.

Priscilla listened attentively, heard every word, and then, after a short pause, as if gathering strength to reply, she fixed her eyes upon the messenger, and said with a frank and pleasant countenance, full of meaning, "Prithee, John, why do you not speak for yourself?" John's ruddy countenance became *red;* he took the hint, made a polite bow, bade farewell for the present, and returned to Standish to communicate the result of his negotiation. Thenceforward he visited for himself, and ere long their nuptials were solemnized in due form, and Miss Priscilla Mullen became Mrs. John Alden. Tradition reports further, that when Alden visited Cape Cod for the purpose of entering into the conjugal relation with Priscilla, as the colony then had no horses, he went mounted on the back of a bull, which he had covered with a piece of handsome broadcloth. After the marriage ceremonies were performed, he relinquished this seat to his new bride. Placing her on the back of the bull, he returned home in joyous triumph, leading the ungainly animal by a rope fastened to a ring in its nose. In relation to this event Thatcher says, "This sample of primitive gallantry would ill compare with that of Abraham's servant, when, by proxy, he gallanted Rebekah on her journey, with a splendid retinue of damsels and servants seated on camels, Isaac going out to meet her. Had the servant employed bulls instead of camels, it may be doubted whether Rebekah would have been quite so prompt in accepting his proposals. As soon as the question was put, Rebekah said, 'I will go.' With equal propriety he might have said, had Mr.

Alden taken a camel instead of a bull, Priscilla Mullens might have declined. They both employed the creature in use among their own people. We are somewhat inclined to the belief, that in each case the lady was influenced more by the man than the animal; more by the home that was offered her, than by the conveyance thither."

We have already intimated, that, after the planting of Plymouth, other settlements were formed in different parts of the country. They increased in numbers and importance. Although they were independent of each other, there were some things in which they had a mutual interest. After the experience of years, it was found desirable, for various reasons, that the colonies which had come into existence in New England, embracing Massachusetts, Plymouth, Connecticut, New Haven, and Saybrook, should unite together upon a common basis, for mutual council, protection, and interest. After spending much time in consultation and correspondence upon the subject, principles of agreement were finally settled, and a CONFEDERATION OF THE NEW ENGLAND COLONIES formed. This was a "perpetual league of friendship and amity, for offence and defence, mutual advice and succor, upon all just occasions, both for preserving and propagating the truths and liberties of the gospel, and for their own mutual safety and welfare." Though the language of the articles of the confederation was not remarkable for its precision, and was susceptible of a liberal construction, yet the interpretation which it generally received, being characterized by sobriety and wisdom, no modification of it was made for thirty years. This may appropriately be regarded as the germ of the American Union. Its immediate effect was to elevate the colonies in respectability and importance, in the estimation of the Dutch, the French, and the Indians. As an insult to one was an insult to the whole ; as all were pledged to defend each, in case of an attack, the neighboring colonies of other nations, as well as the natives, saw that no one plantation could be trifled with or assaulted with impunity. The vengeance of the whole confederation would at once be aroused. Soon after the union was formed, a number of Indian chiefs entered into a friendly alliance with the English, among whom were Miantonomo and Uncas, sagamores of the powerful Narragansetts and the Mohegans.

At one time the project was seriously entertained of removing the colony from Plymouth. The soil was so unproductive, and the location so unfavorable in other respects, that many had left, and others wanted to follow. The question was discussed with much interest in the church. There was, as might be supposed, a wide difference of opinion. Not a few were strongly opposed to the removal, who yet expressed a willingness to acquiesce rather than see the church go to dissolution. A majority was at last obtained in favor of the project. But where shall they go? Different places were proposed; and it may excite a smile when we state that the one selected was Eastham, on Cape Cod, an exposed, barren, and sandy location. It was purchased from the Nauset Indians. But upon more careful examination, it was found to be less desirable than Plymouth. The members of the church changed their purpose, and resolved to remain where they were. There were some exceptions, of persons who could not, or would not, be satisfied with their old location. These bought out the rights of the church to Eastham, removed thither, and commenced a settlement themselves. Thomas Prince, who had been twice governor of the colony, was one of them. What would have been the fate of Plymouth, and of the famous "Rock," if all had removed, we leave the speculative to conjecture.

CHAPTER XVI.

> "Such is our mild and tolerant way,
> We only curse them twice a day,
> According to a form that's set;
> And far from torturing, only let
> All orthodox believers beat 'em,
> And twitch their beards, where'er they meet 'em." — MOORE.

Quakers ordered out of the Colony. — They refuse to obey. — All forbidden to harbor Quakers. — Humphrey Norton imprisoned. — Quakers' Contempt of Government. — Their Insolence to the Governor. — Refuse to take Oath. — Are whipped. — Norton's Letters. — Fanaticism always troublesome. — No Quaker or Ranter permitted to be a Freeman. — A House of Correction ordered to be built. — Six Quakers banished on Pain of Death. — Milder Laws. — Four Persons appointed to reason with them. — One of these becomes a Quaker. — All Persons authorized to arrest them. — Their Meetings forbidden. — Severity excites Sympathy. — Rigorous Measures were not universally approved. — Charles II. ascends the Throne of England. — He suppresses the Persecutions. — Secretary Rawson. — His Daughter Rebecca receives the Attentions of Thomas Rumsey. — Marries him. — Accompanies him to England. — Finds a Relative. — Conduct of her Husband. — Painful Discovery. — Her Abandonment. — Her Self-reliance. — Embarks for Jamaica. — Arrival there. — Her unhappy End.

IT becomes now our painful duty to narrate events, which we would gladly leave untouched, if we could consistently with fidelity. As, however, they are matters of history; as they develop important phases of character, and are prolific in important lessons, they may properly claim a share of our

16*

attention. We refer to the treatment of the Quakers. About 1657, an order was passed, that if any one brought a Quaker, ranter, or other notorious heretic within the jurisdiction of the colony, and should be ordered by a magistrate to return him to the place whence he came, they should obey, or pay a fine of twenty shillings for every week that such obnoxious person remained in the colony after such warning. This, however, was only the beginning of sorrows. In despite of the twenty shilling law, Quakers did come within their precincts and proclaim their hated tenets. This gave occasion for a severer law. It was enacted that no person should harbor or entertain any Quaker in the colony, under a penalty of five pounds for every offence, or a public whipping.

In the month of October, 1657, Humphrey Norton was examined by the court, who found him guilty of "divers horrid errors," and banished him from the colony. He returned, however, in company with another Quaker of similar spirit. They were arrested and imprisoned. A prominent feature in the conduct of the Quakers, which greatly exasperated the court, was their contempt of the legal authorities. They gave their tongues great license, and seem to have imagined that they were honoring God by their insolent defiance of the civil tribunals. Thus, at their examination, Norton said to the governor, a number of times, "Thou liest;" "Thomas, thou art a malicious man." As if determined to provoke severity, he said again to the governor, "Thy clamorous tongue I regard no more than the dust under my feet; and thou art like a scolding woman, and thou pratest and deridest me." As they professed to be English subjects, the court ordered them to take the oath of fidelity to their country. They refused, declaring they would take no kind of an oath. They were then sentenced to be whipped. After the sentence was executed, and whilst they were smarting under the stripes they had received, the marshal ordered them to pay a fee for the whipping! Thatcher says, "In our times, we should think public whipping to be a sufficient punishment, without obliging the culprit to pay the whipper's fee." The fee was probably regarded as a part of the costs of court, which the defaulted party usually pays. Still, it has somewhat the appearance of making a criminal pay the costs of his execution, scaffold and rope included. In this case, however, they refused, and, consequently, were recommitted to prison, where they remained until they compromised the affair with the marshal, when they were released, and left the colony. In order to show the spirit that was cherished, and the language employed on that occasion, by the weaker party, we shall give a few extracts from Norton's letters, written at that time. These are essential to a full view of the facts. In one, addressed to the governor, written just after his punishment, he says, "Thomas Prince, thou hast bent thy heart to work wickedness, and thy tongue hath set forth deceit: thou imaginest mischief upon thy bed, and hatchest thy hatred in thy secret chamber: the strength of darkness is over thee, and a malicious mouth hast thou opened against God and his anointed; and with thy tongue and lips hast thou uttered perverse things: thou hast slandered the innocent, by railing, lying, and false accusations, and with thy barbarous heart hast thou caused their blood to be shed. . . . The curse, causeless, cannot come upon thee, nor the vengeance of God unjustly cannot fetch thee up. . . . The deadly drink of the cup of indignation thou cannot escape, and the grief and cause of travail will not be greater than thine. . . . Thou hast caused to defraud the righteous owner of his goods, and a heaping it up, as upon a hill, wherewith thou wilt purchase to thyself and others a field of blood, wherein to bury your dead. John Alden is to thee like a pack horse, whereupon thou layest thy beastly bag: cursed are all they that have a hand therein. . . . The anguish and pain that will enter thy veins will be like gnawing worms lodging betwixt thy heart and liver. When these things come upon thee, and thy back bowed down with pain, in that day and hour thou shalt know to thy grief that prophets of the Lord we are, and the God of vengeance is our God."

In another to John Alden, less violent in spirit, but of the same general character, he says, "If there be in thee any expectation of mercy, do thou withdraw thy body forever appearing at that beastly bench, where the law of God is cast behind your backs. . . . Let the cursed purse be cast out of thy house, wherein is held the goods of other men."

Both of these letters were signed by Humphrey Norton. The spirit of fanaticism which they exhibit would make men troublesome in any community where they were not restrained by law. In our own day, public worship has been disturbed, and meetings broken up, by men and women who were controlled by similar sentiments. In some instances, they were prosecuted and punished. The difference, however, between these prosecutions and those of the Quakers consists in this: The Quakers were tried and punished for their sentiments; the disturbers of the peace, in our day, are punished, not for their sentiments, but for their unlawful conduct in interfering with the rights and privileges of others.

The next year, it was enacted that no "Quaker, ranter, or any such corrupt person," should be a freeman of the corporation. The court also framed another bill, with this explanatory preamble: "Whereas sundry persons, both Quakers and others, wander up and down in this jurisdiction, and follow no lawful calling to earn their own bread, and also use all endeavors to subvert civil state, and pull down all churches and ordinances of God, to thrust us out of the ways of God, notwithstanding all former laws provided for the contrary." It was therefore ordered that a house of correction be built, in which all such individuals, with all "idle persons, or rebellious children, or servants that are stubborn and will not work," should be obliged to earn their living by labor, under the direction of an overseer.

On the 11th of May, 1659, six persons, among whom were Lawrence Southwick and wife, were sentenced to depart out of the jurisdiction of the colony, by the eighth of June, *on pain of death!* This was a barbarous sentence. We have no evidence, however, that this extreme penalty was inflicted upon any Quaker in the Plymouth colony. For what was done at Boston, in the Massachusetts settlement, they were not responsible. The tragedies which were enacted there, during this period, will be described in another volume on the history of that colony. They would be out of place here.

Later in the year, the laws which were passed against the Quakers at Plymouth assumed a milder character. They authorized the seizure of all books and writings which contained their doctrines, many of which had been circulated throughout the colony. As some of the colonists had been converted to the Quaker belief, it was enacted, that if such would remove out of the government within six months, they should be subjected to no fine ; and those who were too poor to move, should receive assistance at the public expense.

As their next measure for the prevention of the spread of this unwelcome heresy, and for the reclaiming of those who had already embraced it, the government commissioned four individuals to attend the meetings of the Quakers, for the purpose of convincing them of the error of their ways. This was a dangerous experiment. One of those to whom this appointment was given was Isaac Robinson, son of their Leyden pastor, Rev. John Robinson. But in his discussion with the Quakers, instead of convincing them of their errors, they persuaded him that they were truths ; instead of healing the disease, he caught the contagion. They made him a convert. By embracing their sentiments, he rendered himself obnoxious to the government, was dismissed from office, and "exposed to much censure, and some indignity."

In 1660, a law was passed, authorizing all persons to apprehend Quakers, and deliver them to a constable, that they might be brought before the governor or some magistrate for examination. In order to render it difficult for them to itinerate through the colony, in their efforts to disseminate their doctrine, or to escape from the officers of justice, it was enacted "that if any pson or psons shall furnish any of them with horse or horse kind, the same to bee forfeited and seized on, for the use of this Gov^{r}ment; or any horses that they shall bring into the Gov^{r}ment, shalbee brought for them and they make use of, shalbee forfeited, as aforsaid."

The next year it was enacted that if any Quaker came into any of the towns of this government, they should be whipped with rods, not exceeding fifteen stripes, and then have a pass to leave the jurisdiction. If any were found without their pass, or not acting according to it, they should be whipped again. Their meetings were forbidden under a penalty of five pounds to the owner of the premises, or a whipping. Notwithstanding the severity of these enactments, the Quakers multiplied. Sympathy was awakened in their favor. Even the magistrates shrunk from the execution of the laws against them, and finally they resorted again to persuasion, as is evident from the law which was passed to break up their monthly meetings. It was enacted that Mr. Constant Southworth and William Peabody should repair to these meetings, with the marshal, or constable of the town, and use their best endeavors, by argument and discourse, to convince or hinder them.

The statement should not be omitted, that these rigorous measures against the Quakers did not receive the unanimous approval of the government. Mr. Cudworth, Mr. Allerton, Mr. Hatherly, and some others opposed them. The consequence was, they lost their offices as magistrates. A few years, however, produced a great change in public sentiment, and Cudworth, Isaac Robinson, and Hatherly were restored to their offices.

When Charles II. ascended the throne of England, the inhabitants of Plymouth sent to him a declaration of their allegiance. This was soon followed by a *mandamus* from the king commanding the prosecutions against the Quakers to cease, and that those under arrest, whether condemned or not, should be sent to England, with a specification of the crimes alleged against them, that they might be tried according to the laws of the kingdom. This royal mandate was followed by a mitigation of the severities which were practised against them. In Plymouth the most objectionable laws were repealed, and we find no further trace of their persecution. Thus terminated this humiliating and disgraceful affair, the prominent elements of which were heated fanaticism and intolerant bigotry.

During the persecutions of the Quakers in Plymouth, proceedings of even greater severity were instituted against them in the colony of Massachusetts, of which, at that time, Edward Rawson was secretary, who took an active part in their trials. His name frequently appears upon the record of that period as the "Persecutor."

Rawson had twelve children, the history of one of whom is so full of romance and tragedy, as cannot fail to interest the reader; we refer to his daughter, Rebecca. She was a talented young lady, of great personal attractions, and a well-cultivated mind. One of her contemporaries described her as "one of the most beautiful, polite, and accomplished young ladies in Boston." From the position which her father occupied in the government, she doubtless moved in the most elevated circles of colonial society. Among her admirers was a base, unprincipled, deceitful fellow, from England, whose name was Thomas Rumsey, but who passed himself off as Sir Thomas Hale, Jr., nephew to Lord Chief Justice Hale. After an avowal of his passion for the beautiful Rebecca, the mock Sir Thomas ventured to make her proposals of marriage. The young lady, with her other qualities, possessed a good share of "worldly ambition," and regarding the proffer of the young lord a favorable offer, the acceptance of which would introduce her into the fashionable circles of England, and cherishing also tender sentiments towards him, she had no disposition to refuse his hand. Their marriage was solemnized, July 1, 1679, in the presence of about forty persons. This was only the first act of the drama. After receiving the congratulations of her friends, many of whom thought she had been singularly fortunate in the connection, the young bride bade them farewell, and embarked, with her noble husband and a splendid outfit, for the shores of Old England. What hopes and fears, what visions of fancied bliss and forebodings of dreaded evil, passed over her mind, during her long and tedious voyage, we cannot tell. We only know that in due time she, and her handsome outfit, safely arrived. Being anxious to step on the soil of the Empire Isle, she made a hasty toilette, and went on shore "en dishabille," in company with her husband. She succeeded on the second day in finding a relative, with whom they lodged. Sir Thomas, Jr., knowing that the *dénouement* of his nefarious plot was at hand, arose early in the morning, took the keys belonging to his wife, and departed, telling her that he would send the trunks ashore, so that she might dress for dinner. In the course of the morning the trunks came, but as her husband had the keys, they could not be opened. She was obliged to wait for his return. There is a limit to female patience; in her case the limit was soon reached. Whether from any part of his conduct on shipboard, or since their landing, her suspicions were awakened, we know not; but, after waiting impatiently in vain, till two o'clock, for his return, she determined to open the trunks by force. It was done; when, to her amazement, she found every article of clothing, useful and costly, removed, and the trunks filled with worthless combustibles! She was overwhelmed with shame, perplexity, and sorrow. Where her husband had gone, or what had become of her wardrobe, it was equally impossible to tell. The relative with whom she stopped took her in his carriage to the house where she and her husband spent the preceding night. She there inquired for Sir Thomas Hale, Jr. "He has not been here for some days," was the reply.

"He was surely here night before last," said she. They informed her that she was mistaken; that Sir Thomas Hale, Jr., had not been there, but that Thomas Rumsey came there on the night which she had specified, with a young lady. "Where is he now?" "Gone to his wife, in Canterbury." The abominable wickedness of Rumsey and the condition of the unfortunate Rebecca were now fully revealed. She had been deceived and betrayed, and all her hopes of future elevation ruined. She awoke from her dream of pleasure and aggrandizement to a full realization of her humiliating position. Instead of being the lawful wife of a man of honor and title, she found she had been sustaining, ignorantly of course, an illegal connection with a base, licentious fellow, having a wife in England, and who, not satisfied with ruining her, as to her future social prospects, had stripped her of her all, so that she had not even a change of garments. She never saw him again! Being thus robbed and abandoned in a strange land, and having too much spirit to be dependent upon her friends, she threw herself upon her own industry for support. Possessing a good share of natural ingenuity and perseverance, she applied herself so successfully to various kinds of fancy work, that for thirteen years she succeeded in obtaining a "genteel subsistence for herself and child." At the end of this period, she determined to return to her own country. Leaving her child in the care of her sister in England, who had none of her own, she embarked for Jamaica on her way to Boston, in a vessel belonging to her uncle. Her romantic life was here doomed to a tragical end. On the morning of June 9th, 1692, whilst her uncle was on shore, engaged in settling his accounts, and when the vessel was ready to sail for Massachusetts, the island was visited with a tremendous earthquake, which swallowed up the vessel and all on board, among whom was the injured heroine of our story. The uncle was the only one of the ship's company who was saved. Thus terminated the eventful career of the beautiful, accomplished, yet unfortunate Rebecca Rawson. A knowledge of these facts will give a special interest to her likeness in the present volume, which is a copy of her original portrait, now in the possession of R. R. Dodge, East Sutton, Mass.

[illegible]

Born in Boston 1656 Died at Port Royal Jamaica 1692

CHAPTER XVII.

"We have strict statutes, and most biting laws,
The needful bits and curbs to headstrong steeds." — SHAKSPEARE

"The good needs fear no law;
It is his safety, and the bad man's awe." — MASSINGER.

The Enactment of Law develops Character. — Trial by Jury. — Wants of the Colony to be supplied first. — Exports forbidden. — Those who refused the Office of Governor to be fined. — Bradford released by Importunity. — How different now. — Marriage forbidden without the Consent of Parents. — Intentions of Marriage to be published. — Consent of Parents to be obtained to address their Daughters. — Punishment to depend upon the "Quality" of the Offender. — Short Sleeves forbidden. — Laws against Contempt of the Scriptures. — Sabbath-breaking and Gambling Laws executed. — Stocks and Cage always ready. — Psalm Singing. — Courtship punished. — Abuse of Husbands. — Blackbirds' Heads to be obtained. — Effects of Union of Church and State. — Every Colony to have a Church. — Church Rates. — Whales. — Ministers forbidden to leave their People. — Meeting-house in every Town. — Parental Instruction. — Schools. — Arms must be taken to Meeting. — Indians and Wolves. — Effects of these Laws. — The Bible the Basis of their Legislation.

THE character of a people may be learned from their legislation. If the laws of some lost race were to be found, it would not be difficult, though not another word of their annals should be discovered, to ascertain their genius and spirit. The peculiarities of the Puritans are as fully developed in their laws as in any events of their history. Some of their enactments exhibit profound wisdom, sagacity, and forecast; others of them show their strong attachment to the doctrines and precepts of the Bible; whilst another class descend to matters of such trivial nature, as to appear puerile. With reference to this latter class, the Pilgrims acted upon the principle of nipping crime in the bud. The things forbidden may have been, in themselves, comparatively unimportant; but their influence, if unchecked, might have led to gross crimes. By destroying the seeds, they labored to prevent the fruits. Those who wish to go fully into this subject, are referred to the "Charter and Laws of the Colony of New Plymouth," which were collected and published, agreeably to a resolve of the legislature of Massachusetts, in 1836. We shall only give a few of the more important or peculiar of them.

It is an interesting fact, and shows the desire on the part of the colonists to guard the rights of individuals, that the first law on record in the above volume secures trial by a jury consisting of twelve honest men, under oath. This was in 1623. At a later period, 6*d.* was allowed each juror, and 12*d.* to the foreman, as fees.

Three years after, it was enacted that no handicraftsman, as tailors, shoemakers, carpenters, joiners, smiths, or sawyers, belonging to the plantation, should work for any strangers or foreigners, until the necessities of the colony were served.

At the same time, in order to prevent a renewal of the dreadful scarcity which had been previously experienced, the exportation of corn, beans, and peas was prohibited, under the penalty of a confiscation of all such exports.

So small were the honors and emoluments of office, contrasted with its responsibilities, or so limited was the ambition of the Pilgrim fathers, that it seems not to have been an easy thing to find incumbents for the highest stations in the government. Bradford, we know, earnestly desired not to be rechosen governor. He thought the honors and labors of office ought to be distributed. But he was overruled, and kept in. In 1632, it was enacted, that if any were elected to the office of governor, and *would not serve*, he should be fined twenty pounds sterling! If he refused paying the fine, it was to be levied out of his goods or chattels. It was also ordered, that, if any were chosen to the office of council, and declined its acceptance, they should be fined ten pounds each. The only exception specified was in the case of one who should be chosen governor a second time, after having held the office the preceding year. Such a one might decline without the liability of a fine, and then the company were to proceed to a new election, "except they can prevail upon him by entreaty." Governor Winthrop, in his Journal, records in 1633, "Mr. Edward Winslow chosen governor of Plymouth, Mr. Bradford having been governor about ten years, and now by *importunity got off*." What a wonderful contrast does all this present with that unprincipled scrambling for office, that anxiety for public honors and emoluments, with which the country at the present day is so rife! Who now declines the office of governor? In what portion of our land does a necessity exist for a law similar to the above, in order to secure incumbents for the highest local offices?

No persons under "the covert of parents" were allowed to marry without their parents' consent. If this could not be obtained, they were then to get the permission of the governor, or some of his assistants. After which they were to be published three times in a public meeting, or, if no such meetings were held in the town, their intention of marriage was to be posted up in some conspicuous place for fifteen days.

A similar law requiring intentions of marriage to be published fourteen days, including three public days, was in force in Massachusetts, until within a year or two. It became the practice of the editors of some of the daily journals to insert these intentions of marriage in their papers. This, of course, gave greater publicity to the intentions, and was the more repulsive to the parties concerned. After this, many individuals, in order to escape the necessity of giving such notoriety to their private proceedings, would slip into some neighboring state, where they could be united in the "holy bands of matrimony," without any publicity whatever. The law is now altered in Massachusetts. All that is required at present, is to obtain a certificate from the city registrar, or the town clerk, without any previous publication of intention, and the marriage may then be immediately solemnized.

In 1638, it was enacted that if any man offered proposals of marriage to any young lady without *first* obtaining the consent of her parents or master, he should submit to a fine, or to *corporal punishment*, or to both, at the discretion of the court.

Laws were also passed which punished "profane swearing by the name of God, or any of his titles, attributes, word, or works," with a fine of twelve pence for every offence, or exposure in the stocks, not to exceed three hours, or imprisonment "according to the nature and QUALITY OF THE PERSON." It would appear from this, that the degree of punishment was somewhat dependent upon the social position of the offender — the more elevated was the criminal, the heavier the penalty. They did not, however, imitate the example of the Massachusetts colony, who, about the same time, passed the following order, which must have been of special interest to the ladies: "No garment shall be made with short sleeves, and such as have garments with short sleeves shall not wear the same, unless they cover the arm to the wrist; and hereafter, no person whatever shall make any garment for women with sleeves more than half an ell wide," (twenty-two and a half inches.)

Denial of the Scriptures as a rule of life was punishable with whipping. If any "Christian, so called," spoke contemptuously of the Scripture, or of the holy penmen thereof, they were to be punished *by fine or whipping.*

Laws were also passed punishing those who violated the Sabbath — who neglected public worship— who behaved contemptuously towards the minister, the preaching, or the ordinances — who endeavored to subvert the Christian faith by broaching dangerous heresies — who were guilty of drunkenness, of gambling with cards, dice, "cross and pile, or any unlawful game wherein there is a lottery," or of charging too much profit on articles they sold. These laws were not dead letters. It appears as if they were not enacted until there was occasion for them, and then they were carried into execution. We accordingly find that Stephen Hopkins was complained of for selling beer at twopence a quart, which was worth only a penny. Thomas Clark, for selling a pair of boots and spurs for fifteen shillings, for which he gave but ten, was fined thirty shillings.

J. B. was complained of for buying rye at four shillings per bushel, and selling it at five shillings. He was also presented for selling thread at five shillings per pound. The Pilgrims were unwilling that any one should charge an exorbitant profit on what they sold. To a fair remuneration from business they had no objection. They were especially opposed to forestalling.

Nathaniel Bassett and Joseph Prior entered into a church at Duxbury, and disturbed the meeting. They were tried for their offence, and, at the next town meeting, or training day, both were fastened to a post, in some conspicuous place, having upon their heads a paper, on which their crime was written in large letters. A Miss Boulton was guilty of slander. The court condemned her to the humiliating punishment of sitting in the stocks, with a paper fastened to her, written with capital letters, probably containing her crime. John Phillips, for drinking tobacco in the highway, that is, for smoking there, was fined twelve shillings. S. H., for carrying a grist of corn from the mill on Sunday, was sentenced to a fine of twenty shillings, or to be whipped. And W. F., for permitting him to take it from the mill, was fined ten shillings.

J. W. was ordered to be sharply reproved for writing a note on common business, on Lord's day.

John Barnes, for Sabbath-breaking, was sentenced

to a fine of thirty shillings, and to the stocks one hour. William Adey, for a similar offence, received a severe whipping at the post.

In order to be always provided for the immediate execution of these minor penalties, it was ordered that every constablewick should be provided with a pair of stocks, and a cage, of sufficient strength to detain a prisoner. These were continued in use, in different towns, until within the present half century.

Prisoners in the Stocks.

The court authorized Mr. Hatherly to admonish a woman, who had been brought before them, "to be wary of giving offence to others by unnecessary talking." R. B. was summoned to appear and answer for speaking contemptuously of *psalm singing*. He was convicted of the offence. The court sharply admonished him, and ordered him to acknowledge his fault, which he promised to do, and was discharged.

Mr. A. H., for making proposals of marriage to a young lady, Miss E. P., and prosecuting the same contrary to the parents' wishes, and without their consent, and "directly contrary to their mind and will," was sentenced to a fine of five pounds, and to be put under bonds for good behavior, and desist the use of any means to obtain or retain her affections. The bond stated that, "Whereas the said A. H. hath disorderly and unrighteously endeavored to obtain the affections of Miss E. P., against the mind and will of her parents: if, therefore, the said A. H. shall, for the future, refrain and desist the use of any means to obtain or retain her affections, as aforesaid, and appear at court the first Tuesday of July next, and be of good behavior," &c., he shall be released. A. H. did "solemnly and seriously engage before the court, that he will wholly desist, and never apply himself for the future, as formerly he hath done, to Miss E. P., in reference to marriage." He was accordingly released the next July.

Women, for abusing their husbands, or striking their fathers-in-law, were sentenced to be fined or to be whipped at the post.

In town meeting it was ordered that every man in the town procure twelve blackbirds' heads, on pain of paying a fine of two shillings for every default, or twopence apiece for all that fell short of the required number.

It is difficult for us at the present time fully to realize the peculiarity in the practical working of their system, arising from the union of church and state. The leading men in the government were also the influential men of the church. The same act, if committed by a member of the church, would be an offence against both the church and the government, and might subject the offender to a trial before each; and even then, the same individuals would be his judges. In one relation, they would act as government officers; in the other, as members or officers of the church.

Civil and ecclesiastical relations were so interlaced, that the government not only took the church under its protection, but was purposely adjusted to meet her wants. To the Puritans, religion was the most important of all interests, and civil government was valuable in proportion as it secured to them their religious privileges. In their view, the church was like a magnificent temple, and civil government like the scaffolding, useful, mainly, for the assistance which it rendered towards the erection and preservation of that temple. Hence their various legal enactments respecting the constitution of churches, the erection of places of worship, and the support of the ministry.

No new colony was allowed to be planted unless enough joined in it to form a congregation for the observance of public worship; and then the people, if they refused to support their minister voluntarily, were by law assessed, in proportion to their abilities, for his maintenance. For a number of years, these church rates were collected by the minister himself; but as this proved troublesome to the pastor, and gave occasion for prejudice against him, it was enacted, in 1670, that two persons should be appointed to perform this duty. If the people refused payment, the rates were to be obtained by distraint upon their estates.

Occasionally, whales used to be driven ashore and die, when the people would obtain from them their oil. It was enacted at an early period, that when such an incident occurred, or when any whale was cut up at sea, and brought on shore, one full hogshead of oil should be paid to the county. The court also proposed, as a "thing very commendable and beneficial to the towns where God's providence shall cast any whales, if they should agree to set apart some portion of every such fish or oil for the encouragement of an able, godly ministry." It is not improbable that this singular provision was suggested by the fact, that, in ancient times, a whale had been employed for the preservation of a prophet of the Lord. A law was also passed, preventing any pastor or teacher from leaving his church before his complaint had been made known to the magistrates, and they had given both sides a hearing. If the difficulty was owing to the hearers of such minister, the magistrates were to use all "gentle means to upbraid them to do their duty therein." If these were unsuccessful, they were then authorized to employ such other measures "as may put them upon their duty."

In 1675, it was enacted that a meeting-house should be erected in every town in the jurisdiction of the colony. If any town neglected to obey this law, then the governor or the magistrates should appoint persons to build it, according to the wants and the wealth of the people, and charge the expense of it to the inhabitants and proprietors of the town, by whom it should be paid.

Parents were required to see that their children were taught to read the Scriptures, and to recite some short, orthodox catechism, without book; and also, that they were brought up to some honest calling, that would make them useful to themselves and their country.

The towns were advised to obtain a schoolmaster to "train up children to reading and writing." A free school was established, at an expense of thirty-three pounds a year, which expense was to be paid out of the profits of the Cape Cod fishery.

When danger was apprehended from the Indians, every one that went to meeting on Lord's day was ordered to take arms, and at least six charges of powder and shot, under a penalty of two shillings for every omission. At the same time, it was enacted that whosoever "shall shoot off any gun on any unnecessary occasion, or at any game whatsoever, except at an *Indian* or a *wolf*, shall forfeit five shillings for every such shot, till further liberty shall be given."

The enactments which we have now given are sufficient to evince the spirit and character of our Pilgrim fathers. Although some of their laws arrest the attention by their singularity, yet their code, as a whole, was adapted to secure a higher moral character to their community than would have been attained by the adoption of the then existing laws of any other people. With reference to many subjects, they made the Bible the basis of their legislation. They adopted not a few of the moral precepts and the penalties of Moses. It is this which gives an appearance of religious affectation, and even of bigotry, to some of their requirements.

CHAPTER XVIII.

> "Between the acting of a dreadful thing,
> And the first motion, all the interim is
> Like a phantasma, or a hideous dream;
> The genius and the mortal instruments
> Are then in council; and the state of man,
> Like to a little kingdom, suffers then
> The nature of an insurrection." — SHAKSPEARE.

Fifty Years of Peace. — New Settlements. — Converted Indians. — Native Preachers. — Philip and the Button. — Indian Magistrates. — Indian Warrant. — Alexander succeeds Massasoit. — Suspicions against him. — His Death. — Philip becomes Grand Sachem. — Pursues John Gibbs for reviling the Dead. — His Alliance with the Narragansetts. — He desires Revenge. — Ordered to come to Plymouth. — Declines. — Invites the Governor to come to him. — They meet at Taunton. — Singular Scene in a Church. — The Treaty. — Indignant Sachem. — Treaty violated. — Conference at Plymouth. — Indian Confederacy. — Philip's deep Plot against the English. — Their Security. — Philip angry with Sassamon. — The latter flees to the English. — The Plot revealed. — Sassamon missing. — Philip again examined. — No Confession. — Suspicions increase.

AFTER the successful attack of Captain Standish upon the Massachusetts Indians at Weymouth, no other attempts were made against the English by the natives for a period of fifty years. During this time, such was the mutual confidence which was cherished between the two parties, that they not only interchanged visits, and travelled fearlessly through each other's respective jurisdictions, but

Indians dwelt in the colony, and were subject to English laws.

New English settlements were formed in various parts of the different colonies in Massachusetts Bay, on the Connecticut River, and in the neighborhood of Rhode Island. Efforts had also been successful for the instruction and conversion of the natives. Indian churches had been formed at Provincetown, Eastham, Wellfleet, Chatham, Yarmouth, Barnstable, Sandwich, Wareham, Middleborough, and Marshpee. These were the fruits of the Christian zeal and indefatigable perseverance of Richard Bourne, of Sandwich. Through his patient labors, many of these Indians could read and write their own language. They had also received considerable knowledge of the Sacred Scriptures. Four of them had made such progress in Christian knowledge, that they were approbated as preachers to their own tribes, and labored as Mr. Bourne's assistants. In 1685, there were fourteen hundred and thirty-nine converted Indians in the colony. They were generally called "praying Indians."

Conversions were effected at Martha's Vineyard and Nantucket, through the instrumentality of Thomas Mayhew. So successful were the missionary efforts of this man of God, that on the Island of Martha's Vineyard, six meetings were held in different places, every Sabbath. There were ten native preachers, who, according to Mayhew's testimony, were of "good knowledge and holy conversation." Nearly all the natives in the colony of Massachusetts had embraced Christianity. They had been favored with the instructions of the apostle Eliot. Many of the natives resisted all attempts at their conversion. Massasoit, though a firm friend to the English, obstinately refused to abandon the religion of his fathers. Philip, his son, on one occasion, after listening to the religious exhortation and reasonings of Eliot, took that apostle by the button, and said, "I care no more for the gospel than you do for that button." This was the feeling of a large number. The Narragansetts went so far as actually to prohibit the preaching of the gospel within their borders.

After the Indians had been suitably instructed, some of the more intelligent and energetic of them received appointments to different offices, as petty judges, or as constables. With such commissions they were highly pleased, and sometimes would discharge their official duty with amusing formality. The following warrant, directed to an Indian constable, was issued by one of these native magistrates. It furnishes an example of sententious brevity, in wide contrast with the verbosity of more civilized legal formulas. : —

"I, Hihoudi, you, Peter Waterman, Jeremy Wicket, quick you take him, fast you hold him, straight you bring him before me. Hihoudi."

After the death of Massasoit, his son, Alexander, became his successor. His career, however, was short. The English were informed that he was plotting their destruction. He was, therefore, ordered to come to Plymouth and answer this charge. He promised to comply, but did not. His refusal, which involved a violation of his promise, strengthened the suspicions against him. The governor ordered Major Josiah Winslow to take a company of armed men, and bring him to Plymouth. This posse set out and fortunately came upon Alexander, with a small party of his men, when they were busily engaged in eating. They were in a house, or tent, and their guns carelessly left on the outside. Winslow first secured their guns, and then, in the name of the government of Plymouth, ordered the chief to accompany him to the colony. He consented and went, but was soon after taken sick, and died.

He was succeeded by his brother Philip, as grand sachem of the Pokanoket, or Wampanoag Indians. His residence was at Mount Hope, which is supposed to be a corruption of Montaup. He, and also his brother before him, renewed the alliance of friendship with the English, which their father had originally made. It is related of him, that in 1665 he went to Nantucket with his braves, for the purpose of killing an Indian who had spoken contemptuously of Massasoit, his father, as it was a law among them that whoever reviled the dead should suffer death. The offender was one John Gibbs, a "praying Indian" and Christian preacher, whose church numbered about thirty members. Gibbs, being informed by a friend of Philip's design, fled. Philip caught a sight of the fugitive, and followed him through the town, from house to house, until Gibbs leaped a high bank, eluded his sight, and made his escape. When the English in the place were informed of the facts, they sought an interview with the offended chief. They were anxious to save the life of the offender. As, however, the offence was regarded as a grave affair by the Indians, Philip refused to return until the English agreed to ransom the criminal for nineteen shillings, that being all the money there was on the island. He then returned home satisfied.

Philip frequently visited Plymouth. He became well acquainted with the inhabitants, traded with them, and exchanged hospitalities. Yet it is supposed that all this time the insult which had been offered to his brother Alexander was rankling in his heart, and calling for revenge.

In addition to the supposed injury done to Alexander, as Philip was in general alliance with the Narragansetts, he must have sympathized with them in the aggressions which were, from time to time, made upon them by the English. Between them and the colonists difficulties had repeatedly occurred. To Philip, it appeared that, in these difficulties, his Indian friends were wronged. He espoused their side, and no doubt labored to deepen their sense of injury from the whites. As at that time there seems to have been, among the Narragansetts, no chief who had supreme command over the whole tribe, although there were several sachems who had their respective followers, they were the more willing to avail themselves of the prowess and skill of Philip, to manage for them their cause. These two things — the treatment of Alexander and of the Narragansetts by the English — are believed to have been the original causes of Philip's bloody war.

In 1671, he began to manifest a quarrelsome disposition. He complained of English encroachments. His followers frequently met together, repaired their muskets, sharpened their tomahawks, and used irritating language to the English.

A message was sent to Philip to come to Plymouth and explain his conduct. To this command he paid no attention. He afterwards reciprocated this courtesy, and invited the governor of Plymouth to hold a conference with him. In his reply the governor assured him of his willingness to hold a conference, but expected that Philip would come to him at Taunton, where he then was. The chief refused.

After considerable negotiation through the medium of messengers, one of whom was Roger Williams, Philip agreed to meet him at the place designated. The conditions on which the chief consented to come to Taunton were, that his men should accompany him, and that the conference should take place in the meeting-house ; the two parties to occupy the opposite sides of the house. Here they accordingly met. Such a congregation, and for such a purpose, had never assembled there before. On one side of the church were arrayed the Puritans, with their round heads, occasioned by the close cutting of their hair, their "formal garb," and their stern, serious features; on the other side were the Indians, with their long dark hair streaming over their shoulders or down their backs, arrayed in skins, blankets, and calicoes, and decorated in taudry style, with beads, wampum, feathers, and various gay colors. It was a scene of singular appearance. If the agreement then formed had been faithfully fulfilled, it would have been a conference of great importance, and would have prevented the shedding of much blood.

Philip denied the charges which were brought against him, and said that his warlike preparations were intended for an attack upon the Narragansetts. But when it was shown that he was on more friendly relations with the Narragansetts than usual, and that he had arranged plans of attack upon Seekonk, Taunton, and some other towns, he saw that his conspiracy was discovered, and that there was no way of disproving it. Up to this time he had managed every thing with so much secrecy, that he had not the least suspicion that his plot was detected. He was therefore confounded when the English brought forward their evidence against him. Knowing that it would be just for them to punish him for his treachery, and fearing, perhaps, that they might execute summary vengeance upon him, he willingly consented to sign a document, containing a confession of his guilt, a renewal of his allegiance to the English, and a readiness to deliver up all his English weapons into their hands, to be kept as long as they should think it necessary. When the Indians understood the terms of his submission, one of his sachems was so indignant at his cowardice, that he angrily threw his weapons on the ground, abandoned his cause forever, and immediately identified himself with the Puritans, to whom he continued a faithful adherent during the whole of this sanguinary war.

After the negotiations were over, and the parties had separated, Philip failed to comply with the terms imposed upon him. He sent in no weapons. The truth is, he had no intention to. He signed that submission only to save his life. Once free from the English, he thought of his promise no more. Chiefs and braves of other tribes now united with him. His conduct continuing suspicious, the colony of Plymouth summoned him again to appear there. They also sent word to the colony of Massachusetts of what they had done, and stated that if Philip did not appear, and the government of Massachusetts did not satisfactorily account for his refusal, force would be used to compel his attendance ; and, as it was common cause, Massachusetts ought to unite with them ; but if they refused, then Plymouth would enter upon the contest alone. The same day on which that letter reached Boston, Philip himself arrived there. He succeeded in convincing the government there that he cherished no unfriendly designs against Plymouth. They proposed to Plymouth that the difficulties should be referred for adjustment to commissioners, to be appointed by the governments of Massachusetts and Connecticut. After some hesitation, this plan was acceded to, and the commissioners appeared at Plymouth, where Philip also presented himself. The result of this conference was another treaty, in which Philip promised to pay the government of Plymouth one hundred pounds of such things as he had ; to refer all differences between his people and the English to the Plymouth government, and not to engage in any war without their approbation. After this, no collision occurred between the two parties for three years. Yet Philip was not subdued, neither did he relinquish his murderous designs against the English. During these three years of apparent friendliness, he was engaged in bringing about a confederacy of all the Indian tribes in New England, for the purpose of an entire extermination of the English colonies. To accomplish this, he had to perform the difficult task of terminating quarrels of long standing between different tribes; of allaying the enmity between different chiefs; of answering objections, removing difficulties, and effecting a harmonious union between elements of the most discordant nature. Yet all this he had the consummate address successfully to accomplish. During all this period, while the train was being prepared for a terrific explosion, the English were kept in profound ignorance. Philip was strengthening his forces, multiplying his alliances, and extending his plan of operations, whilst those who were to be his victims were lulled into a sense of perfect security by his peaceful appearance and his false professions of friendship. Had his treachery been kept concealed until the time appointed for the attack upon the colonies, which was the spring of 1676, we know not how the entire overthrow of the English plantations could have been prevented. But this was not to be. The vine which had been brought out of Egypt, and transplanted into this distant soil, was under the protection of an omniscient and all-powerful Friend: no evils plotted against it were unknown to him — no power opposed to it which he could not defeat. Though now, the boar out of the wood and the wild beasts of the field were intent upon devouring it, yet his hand held them in check as with bit and bridle, and his providence led to a discovery of the dangers which encompassed it.

Among the confidential Indians of Philip was one John Sassamon, whom he employed as his secretary. By some offence, this individual aroused the anger of Philip. He had previously been under the instruction of Eliot, and was professedly converted to the Christian faith. But after residing a while with Philip, he abandoned his profession. Having offended his chief, and fearing his anger, he fled to his old friend, Eliot. The venerable missionary received him with his accustomed kindness, and entered into conversation with him respecting his religious state. His pious heart earnestly longed to see the apostate take his old place, and manifest his former religious interest among the "praying Indians." His faithful and affectionate labors for the restoration of the prodigal were crowned with success. "After many professions of repentance, he was *again baptized* and received into full communion."

It was so ordered by a wise Providence, that the Indian who was, in this manner, obliged to flee from home, was acquainted with both the designs and the plans of Philip. Being now fully devoted to the interests of the English, Sassamon, in a secret manner, made known to the governor of Plymouth Philip's treachery, at the same time informing him, that if Philip should ever learn that he had betrayed him, it would cost him his life. After the reception of this fearful intelligence, Philip and some of his tribe were examined; but as they made no confessions, and as no positive evidence was brought against them, they were discharged, — not, however, without having the suspicions against them greatly strengthened. It was not long before poor Sassamon mysteriously disappeared — in what manner will be related in the next chapter.

CHAPTER XIX.

> "His savage hordes the murderous *Philip* leads,
> Files through the woods, and treads the tangled weeds;
> Shuns open combat, teaches where to run,
> Skulk, couch the ambush, aim the hunters' gun,
> Whirl the sly tomahawk, the war-whoop sing,
> Divide the spoils, and pack the scalps they bring." — BARLOW.

Harvard College. — Indian Students. — Sassamon. — Search for him. — His Body found. — Murderers arrested and executed. — Philip enraged. — Preparations for Conflict. — Bold Language. — Opinion respecting the first Fire. — Indians pant for Plunder. — The War begun. — English killed on Fast Day. — Excitement in the Colonies. — Enlisting Recruits in Boston. — Bridgewater Horsemen. — People driven from their burning Houses. — The English surprised and slain. — Affecting Scene. — Philip pursued. — Found at Dinner. — Escapes. — Mutilated Englishmen. — Fuller's narrow Escape. — Church's brave Adventure. — Golding's timely Arrival. — Marvellous Preservation. — Church's Visit to the Spring amidst a Shower of Balls.

PREVIOUS to the events contained in the last chapter, Harvard College had been founded, consecrated to Christ and his church. Efforts were early made to induce some of the Indian youth to prepare to enter. These efforts were not favored with much success. The restraints of a student's life were not at all in harmony with the freedom of their early habits. They greatly preferred to be rambling the fields and woods, with their bow and arrows, for game, or paddling their light bark canoes over the water for fish, or spending their time in idle talk, or useless sports, to the stillness, confinement, and monotony of intellectual pursuits. Yet, now and then one could be induced to enter; among these was Sassamon. He received a tolerable education, was well acquainted with the English language, and had been employed as a preacher among the Indians, and as a teacher of their youth. Soon after the disclosures which Sassamon made to the governor of Plymouth, he was missing! When he left, or where he had gone, no one knew. Fears were entertained for his safety. It was suspected that he had been murdered. His friends commenced a thorough search for him. Every cave, brook, woods, or dark corner, where they imagined it was possible for him to be concealed, was closely examined. It was not long before they got upon his track. A hat and gun, which were recognized as his, were found upon a frozen pond in Middleborough. This led to a close examination of the pond itself. Under the ice was discovered the body of a man. Being drawn ashore, it was found to be Sassamon himself. It was evident, from bruises upon him, that he had not died by simply falling through the ice. Cotton Mather states that the neck was broken. Still, he was buried by his friends. But when the appearance of the body was made known to the governor of Plymouth, he, recollecting the fears which Sassamon had expressed respecting himself, gave orders to have his body exhumed and examined. It was done; and bruises enough were found upon him to have caused death without drowning. An Indian now acknowledged that he saw him murdered, but had not made the disclosure, for fear he should lose his own life. The accused persons were apprehended, removed to Plymouth, and tried. The jury consisted of twelve Englishmen, and four grave, impartial, judicious Indians. The criminals, being three in number, were all convicted, and paid the penalty of death. Dr. I. Mather says, that "when Tobias, one of the culprits, came near the body, it fell a bleeding on fresh, as it had been newly slain; albeit it was buried a considerable time before that." A notion, which we cannot help characterizing as superstitious, prevailed at that time, that when a murderer touched or approached a body which he had slain, the wounds would send forth fresh blood. Whether this phenomenon, stated by Mather, had any effect with the jury, we know not. At the present day, it would be discarded. One of the criminals confessed the murder; the others, to the last, denied all participation and all knowledge of it.

Philip was greatly enraged at the execution, and longed for the hour of revenge. He had succeeded in forming an alliance with a number of tribes, the young men of which were anxious for plunder, scalps, and war. Whilst both parties were preparing for the approaching bloody conflict, the governor of Massachusetts sent a messenger to Philip, to ask his reasons for wishing to make war with the English, and also to invite him to enter into a new treaty. The bold chieftain of the forests sent back by the messenger this independent reply: "Your governor is but a subject of King Charles of England. I shall not treat with a subject. I shall treat of peace only with the king, my brother. When he comes, I am ready." Professing to be a king, he would negotiate only with a king.

As Philip's designs had been disclosed to the English, he was unable to consummate all the arrangements which he had contemplated prior to the open development of his plans. It was his intention that the first intelligence of his murderous object should have reached the English through the sharp crack of his musket, and the red glare of their burning dwellings. As it was, he was obliged to commence the war prematurely, and under great disadvantages. A notion prevailed among the Indians, that the party who should begin hostilities by firing the first gun would be defeated. It was their policy, therefore, to insult and irritate the English, so that they might give the first fire. Philip had gathered such large numbers of Indians of different tribes around him, who were panting for scalps and plunder, and who were nourishing their warlike aspirations by the recital of the deeds of blood of their fathers, that it was difficult to prevent them from rushing upon the Puritans, and murdering them whenever they had opportunity. He finally consented that they might kill the cattle of the English, and rob them of their property. After receiving this permission, they prowled around the people of Swansey, killed their cattle, plundered their houses, and menaced them with insulting language. An Englishman was so indignant at their conduct, that, under the impulse of his excited feelings, he seized his musket, fired, and wounded an Indian. This was just what the savages wanted — what they had been endeavoring to provoke. The foreigners had fired the first gun: they were the party to be defeated. The report of that musket was the signal for attack, whenever and wherever the English could be found. It was upon a day of "public humiliation, fasting, and prayer" that this dreadful tragedy began.

The echo of this "first gun" had scarcely died away, before the Indians had prepared themselves to give the Puritans, on their return from meeting, a warm reception. When they made their appearance, and came within reach of the guns, the savages fired upon them, killing one and wounding two! Two others, who were going after a physician, were also met and slain. In another part of the town six more were overtaken, and fell a sacrifice to the vengeance of the Indians the same day. This little, isolated band of settlers were filled with consternation. They were separated so far from Plymouth and Boston, that if the Indians were to come down upon them in overwhelming numbers, they could exterminate the whole before help could possibly arrive. They immediately, however, sent off couriers to the parent settlements. These messengers, filled with anxiety and sorrow, hastened on with as much rapidity as was consistent with vigi lance and safety. When they arrived and communicated the sad intelligence, it produced great commotion. It was understood to be the breaking out of a bloody Indian war. The drums beat; recruits were ordered; and at Boston, in the space of three hours, one hundred and ten men enlisted, under the command of Captain Samuel Mosely. There were also about a dozen privateers who accompanied them, taking with them several dogs. These dogs proved of considerable service in discovering the hiding-places of the Indians. One of them assisted in supplying the party with meat, by going out for several days in succession, and bringing in from six to ten pigs belonging to Philip's herds.

At Plymouth, the governor gave orders that twenty horsemen, well armed, should be raised in Bridgewater, and proceed at once to Swansey. It was done. On their way to the scene of action, they met the terrified people who had been driven from their burning houses, and were fleeing in dismay, "wringing their hands, and bewailing their losses."

Before the help arrived, the inhabitants of Swansey and Rehoboth had collected together in three houses, taking with them such provision as they were able to collect in haste. Here were gathered men, women, and children. The husbands, fathers, and friends of some of them had been slain. They were in deep distress, and trembling with apprehension lest greater calamities would befall them. They were not mistaken. A company of the men left the little garrison, and, taking with them some carts, went to a house which had been deserted, in order to get a quantity of corn, which had there been left. They were met by a friend, who advised them to return, as the Indians were on the alert, and would probably attack them. Paying no attention to this judicious advice, they pressed on, were surprised by a band of natives, fired upon, and six were either killed on the spot, or mortally wounded! The report of the guns was heard at the garrison. It came like the knell of death. They feared that some were killed; but who, they were yet to learn. The soldiers immediately hastened to the spot; but when they arrived, the Indians had scattered and disappeared like the smoke of their muskets. When the soldiers returned, bringing the wounded and the dead with them, and wives, children, and friends gathered in agony around the bleeding or lifeless bodies of those whom they loved, it added greatly to the horrors of their condition. They remained there until reënforcements arrived, when they were safely conducted to Rhode Island.

Soldiers were now sent off in pursuit of Philip, as he was the evil genius of the war. They came upon him so suddenly as to find him at his dinner. Without stopping to apologize, he arose and fled. The soldiers pursued him with such vigor, that he lost his cap, which fell into the hands of one of the pursuers. In this hot and rapid chase, fifteen or more of his adherents were shot. When the pursuers returned, they took all his cattle, swine and corn, and disposed of them at their pleasure. Their joy, however, over the recent success was checked, when they discovered the heads of eight Englishmen, who had been slain, fixed upon poles. They removed them, and gave them an interment. In some instances, other parts of the mutilated bodies were also found. They now explored the country around Philip's residence. They found the houses of the English burnt, their property plundered, and their blood shed, where any of them had, unfortunately, been found by the savages. When they came upon any Indians, a skirmish ensued, and the savages were repulsed. After a thorough exploration of the woods and swamps around Mount Hope, they were satisfied that Philip had fled. Believing they should find him at Pocasset, they went thither. There a party of the English, under Captain Fuller, were attacked by a much larger company of the enemy. The English retreated hastily to the sea-shore, took possession of a house near the water, from which they successfully embarked in a sloop, and escaped to Rhode Island. Captain Church, who had accompanied them, passed down into a point of land, at the south of Tiverton, where he came upon a body of several hundred savages, who attacked him with great fury. The desire of the Indians was to surround them, when, in all probability, they would have cut them entirely off. As soon as Church discovered their design, he gave orders to retreat to the shore. This movement finally resulted in the deliverance of his little gallant band, who numbered less than twenty. With the water before them, and hundreds of their enraged enemies in pursuit, it appeared as if nothing remained for them but to part with their lives as dearly as possible. The Indians had taken shelter behind every tree, bush, fence, or rock, from which they poured their fire into the English. Church, being a man of great courage, was successful in imparting something of the same spirit to his disheartened men. They got behind piles of stones, and experienced many narrow escapes. Orders had been given for boats to attend them ; but they run aground, and so could not extend any relief. Finally one got afloat, and approached towards them. As they saw it advancing, their hopes of deliverance revived. The Indians saw it also, and by firing at it, kept it at such a distance as to be of no service. Church gave them orders to get out of the reach of the muskets, and then send their canoe to take them on board. But the men being fearful to do even this, Church, under apparently feelings of great irritation, ordered them off, or he would fire upon them. They obeyed, and left the English in greater peril than before. After the boat left, the Indians were encouraged, and poured in their balls "thicker and faster than before." The sun was now nearly set, the gloom of evening was arriving, the ammunition of the English was nearly gone, the men exhausted with hunger, excitement, and fighting, whilst the Indians had succeeded in getting possession of a stone house, in which they were sheltered. Down to the present time not one of the English had been shot. Just before dark a sloop made her appearance. Church told the men to hold on, for relief was at hand. He informed them that the captain of the sloop was named Golding, "whom he knew to be a man for business."

He was right. When Golding arrived, he at once sent his canoe ashore; but it proved to be such a diminutive affair that only two could embark in it. As, however, there were no other means of escape, the retreat was made in this. As the English passed to and fro, between the sloop and the shore, the Indians kept up their fire upon them. After Church had seen all the others on board, he embarked himself. The balls whistled around him; one grazed his head; two others entered the canoe, and another was buried in a stake, which was just "in front of the middle of his breast." The battle had continued six hours, during which a number of the Indians were killed; but, as a kind Providence would have it, the English were marvellously preserved. So effectually had the enemy fired upon the sloop, that her sails, colors, and stern were full of holes.

Church was a brave man, and exhibited on that day feats of noble daring. During the fight, being extremely thirsty, he left his shelter, and went fearlessly to a spring and drank; as he returned, he left his hat and cutlass behind him. Towards the evening, when the retreat was made, he remembered these forgotten articles, and being unwilling that the savages should get them, and glory over them as trophies, he went out again, with his musket presented, to obtain them. When the Indians saw it, they let fly a volley of balls upon him; but he pressed on, secured the desired articles, returned and took his seat in the canoe, without receiving a single wound.

After these adventures, the companies under Church and Fuller were again united.

CHAPTER XX.

"Cold with the beast he slew, he sleeps;
O'er him no filial spirit weeps.
E'en that he lived is for his conqueror's tongue;
By foes alone his death-song must be sung;
No chronicles but theirs shall tell
His mournful doom to future times;
May these upon his virtues dwell,
And in his fate forget his crimes." — SPRAGUE.

Philip retreats to a Swamp. — An Ambush. — Wigwams found. — Philip escapes by Water. — His Route discovered. — Ministers fight. — Philip overtaken. — A Battle ensues. — The War becomes general. — Its Consequences. — Disgraceful Conduct towards the Dartmouth Indians.— Sold into Slavery.— Its Influence on other Tribes. — Philip's Ravages in Plymouth. — Retreats to a Swamp. — The Swamp surrounded. — Philip shot. — The Enemy routed. — The Gun preserved. — Philip beheaded and quartered. — His Head and Hand preserved. — Bitter Spirit of the English. — His Head exposed many Years.

AFTER the engagements which were mentioned in the last chapter, the courage of the English was increased. They desired to follow after Philip until they found him. Church went to Narraganset, obtained some more men, returned and found Philip, with whom he had an encounter, and slew fifteen of his men. Philip then retreated into a great swamp, near Taunton River. He was pursued by the English, who penetrated into the swamp, where they were drawn into an ambush. The wily savages fired upon them from behind trees, bushes, and other places of concealment; and five, some accounts say fifteen, men were slain. Near the edge of this swamp a hundred wigwams were found, made of green bark. They attempted to burn them, but could not succeed. In one of them was an old Indian, who informed them that Philip was concealed in the swamp. This intelligence prompted them to greater exertions. But as night was approaching, and friend could not be told from foe, the English retreated, taking their dead and wounded with them. As it was, it is not impossible that they mistook friends for enemies, and thus killed some of their own company. Doctor Mather says, "It is verily feared that the English themselves did unhappily shoot Englishmen instead of Indians."

The forces of the English were now divided. A portion of them remained to watch Philip in the swamp, and starve him into submission. They invested the swamp thirteen days, during which time Philip and his men were diligently employed in making bark canoes. At the end of this period, he and his warriors succeeded in making their escape by water, which bounded a portion of the great swamp. In effecting this flight, they probably used the canoes which they had made during their imprisonment. Their women and children they left behind, as they knew it was the custom of the English to treat such with kindness. A broken, hilly country affords special facilities for the concealment of a retreating army. By following the course of the valleys, and sending their scouts cautiously to the tops of the hills, for the purpose of discovering the safest route, an escape may readily be secured without detection. Philip, however, was not favored with such a country. The land through which he and his followers were obliged to pass, after crossing Taunton River, was level. It afforded no means of concealment, and, consequently, he was discovered. As soon as his course was known, Rev. Mr. Newman, of Rehoboth, called upon his fellow-townsmen with earnestness to pursue him. He set the example himself. Taking his weapons he sallied out, and, by means of spirited addresses, succeeded in diffusing something of his own courage into the company which followed. It was not unusual in those times, when the English were liable to be attacked with suddenness, and with overwhelming numbers, for the ministers of the Prince of peace to gird on the weapons of war, and go out to protect their homes, their wives, and their children. Mr. Newman's company was joined by a party of fifty Mohegan Indians, who had offered their services to Massachusetts, and were placed under the command of Captain Henchman. The little army hastened on and overtook Philip about ten o'clock, A. M., on the first of August.

An engagement at once took place. The balls flew with fatal effect. Philip brought some of his bravest men in the rear so as to be nearest their pursuers, by which means many of them were slain, among whom was Sachem Nimrod, called in the Indian tongue Woonashum, a brave warrior and sagacious counsellor. For some cause which has not been satisfactorily explained, the fight suddenly terminated, and the pursuit was stopped. It was said, at the time, that some of the Mohegans found a quantity of plunder, and whilst they stopped to load themselves with it, Philip made his escape. The extreme heat of the weather has been assigned as another reason; neither of which are satisfactory. Had Philip at that time been closely pursued, the war might have been terminated in a short period, and many lives saved. The Indians were now every where in arms against the English. Men left their homes in the morning to work in the fields, and never returned alive. They were shot down by some invisible foe. Women, left at home, were assaulted by bands of prowling Indians, and after submitting to every species of brutal insult, were butchered in cold blood. The darkness of the night would be suddenly lighted up by the glare of their burning barns. If the owners left their house to extinguish it or to save their cattle, they would be met by the fatal ball. Not satisfied with burning barns, or killing cattle, they would kindle dwelling-houses, and then shoot the inhabitants as they attempted to escape. The dwellings of the English were every where barricaded, and put in as strong a state of defence as possible. Still the Indians were greatly successful. Not only were the isolated houses consumed, and the families slain, but town after town fell before them, and the inhabitants slaughtered without mercy.

As the seat of war was now transferred from the limits of Plymouth colony, we must reserve the further accounts of it until we take up the histories of the colonies into which it was removed.

We have reserved till now the recital of an act of deception, perfidy, and cruelty on the part of the English, which has justly brought upon them eternal disgrace. Soon after the breaking out of the war, the town of Dartmouth was destroyed, and many of the inhabitants slain. In this destruction and slaughter, the Dartmouth Indians had no hand. When the Plymouth forces arrived there, they opened negotiations with these Indians. By the persuasions and promises of Ralph Earl and Captain Eels, they yielded themselves prisoners to the English, and were taken to Plymouth. The question was then discussed, What shall be done with them? It was proposed to sell them into slavery! Against this, Eels, Church, and Earl remonstrated in the strongest manner, and dwelt with emphasis on the promises they had made the Indians, as an inducement to submit. Their earnest and solemn protests produced no effect. The government, notwithstanding the inhumanity and wickedness of the act, gave orders for the whole of them to be sold into slavery! In compliance with the order, these one hundred and sixty Indians were conveyed out of the country. Church was so indignant at such perfidious conduct, and expressed himself with such warmth and bitterness, that the government never forgave him.

The influence of this act was, as it ought to have been, prejudicial to the interests of the Puritans. Baylies says: "This mean and treacherous conduct alienated all the Indians who were doubting, and even those who were strongly disposed to join the English."

After many of the towns in the other colonies had been plundered and destroyed, Philip returned to Plymouth, and continued his ravages there. Various settlements in the colony were attacked, burnt, and the inhabitants slaughtered, with all the cruelties of Indian barbarity. Finally, Philip retreated to a swamp. This was so completely surrounded by English volunteers, under Church, as to cut off all possibility of escape. If Philip showed himself at the edge, he was immediately driven back by the muskets of the English. Captain Church ordered

Golding to enter the swamp. When Philip found himself closely pursued, he retreated to the other side of the swamp; there he was met by Caleb Cook, and a friendly Indian, named Alderman. Cook aimed first at Philip, but his gun only snapped. Alderman then levelled his piece, which was loaded with two balls, and fired. Philip sprang from the ground, and fell upon his face, in the mud and water, dead. One of the balls pierced his heart; the other entered his lungs.

The successful champion immediately informed Captain Church of Philip's death. Church ordered him to keep it secret until they had swept the swamp clear of the enemy. This was soon done. The little English band were then assembled together at the place where the enemy had spent the night, and there Church communicated the welcome news of Philip's death, at which the whole company gave three loud, hearty cheers. The captain ordered the body of the slain chief to be produced; upon which, some of Church's Indians went to the place, seized Philip by the legs, and drew him "through the mud into the upland; and a doleful, great, naked, dirty beast he looked like."

Thus died King Philip, one of the sons and successors of the great Massasoit, and the most dangerous enemy with which the New England colonists were obliged to contend.

His body, in accordance with the barbarous custom of the times, was beheaded, quartered, and exposed as a warning to others. A day of thanksgiving for this signal victory was appointed at Plymouth, and on that day the head of Philip was taken there, accompanied with demonstrations of triumph and great joy. It was elevated in a conspicuous place, and remained publicly exposed above twenty years.

After the death of Philip, Cook persuaded Alderman to exchange guns, so that he might have some memento of this great exploit. This gun was preserved in the family until the present century. The lock was then removed from it, and given to the late Isaac Lothrop, Esq., of Plymouth. The stock and barrel of the gun are said to be still in the possession of Cook's descendants. There is a gun lock in the library of the Massachusetts Historical Society, which is said to be the same which belonged to the gun when it sent the fatal ball into Philip's heart. Alderman, being desirous of preserving some trophy of his victory for himself, cut off one of Philip's hands, which was greatly scarred by the bursting of a pistol, preserved it in rum, and afterwards exhibited it to the people throughout the country, for which he received a small gratuity.

During this war, the English manifested a very bitter spirit against the Indians. This, of course, was to be expected. Dr. Increase Mather, when speaking of the benefit of prayer against Philip, says, "Nor could they cease crying to the Lord until they had prayed the bullet into his heart." At another time, when speaking of the death of some of Philip's people at Narraganset, his language was, "We have heard of two and twenty Indian captains slain, all of them brought down to hell in one day." In the year 1700, he wrote, "It was not long before the hand which now writes, upon a certain occasion, took off the jaw from the exposed skull of that blasphemous leviathan; and the renowned Samuel Lee hath since been a pastor to an English congregation, sounding and showing the praises of heaven upon that very spot of ground where Philip and his Indians were lately worshipping the devil." It would seem, from this, that the skull of this famous Indian chieftain was exposed about twenty-five years.

CHAPTER XXI.

> "A valiant man
> Ought not to undergo or tempt a danger
> But worthily, and by selected ways.
> He undertakes by reason, not by chance." — BEN JONSON.

> "The wise and active conquer difficulties,
> By daring to attempt them. Sloth and folly
> Shiver and shrink at sight of toil and hazard,
> And make the impossibility they fear." — ROWE.

The War not ended. — Annawon holds out. — Prowls around the Towns. — Church goes in Pursuit. — Captures a Party of Indians. — Man seeking his Father. — Church discovers a Path. — Takes an old Indian and young Girl. — Examines them. — Learns Annawon's Retreat. — Old Man becomes Guide. — He refuses to fight against his Chief. — Leads them to Annawon's Encampment. — High Rock. — Exciting Scene. — Church's Stratagem. — Its Execution. — Annawon surprised. — The whole Band captured. — Leaders cannot sleep. — Philip's Ornaments delivered up. — Church's Anxiety. — Morning. — Prisoners taken to Plymouth. — What shall be done with them? — Opinion of Ministers. — Young Annawon. — Prisoners sold into Slavery. — Church opposed to it.

THE death of Philip did not terminate the war. Some of the chiefs who had been his adherents were disposed to hold out against the English somewhat longer; among these, none were more notorious, or more feared, than Annawon. He was bold, cunning, and cruel. He had slain many of the English, some of whom were put to death with tortures. Captain Church, having been informed,

21 *

after the death of Philip, that Annawon was prowling around Rehoboth and Swansey, inflicting all the injury in his power, and being requested by the government to go in pursuit of him, consented. His adventures on this occasion are among the most remarkable which occurred during this memorable war. Church took with him Mr. Jabez Howland, another Englishman by the name of Cook, and six friendly Indians. This was all the force he had with which to conquer some fifty or sixty bold warriors, commanded by one of Philip's bravest and most sagacious captains, at a time when they were smarting from recent wounds, irritated by their late defeat, and burning to revenge the death of their recently slaughtered chief and companions.

Unmindful of the strength which would be arrayed against them, this little band advanced boldly into the enemy's country. It was not long before the scouts discovered a party of Annawon's men, and captured them. This was an encouraging omen. The captain inquired where he would find their chief. They gave him to understand that that was a difficult matter ; as, in order to escape detection, he changed his lodgings every night.

One of the Indians who had accompanied Church asked permission to go in search of his father, who was in a swamp, only a few miles from the place where they then were, with no other company than a young squaw. Church gave him permission, but concluded to go with him, in hopes of getting track of Annawon. Taking with him a few of the party, he set out, leaving Howland behind. When they arrived at the swamp, he sent the Indian on to find his father. Whilst he was gone, Church succeeded in discovering a narrow path, which led from a forest in the vicinity down to the swamp. Believing it to have been made by Indians, he ordered his men to conceal themselves, some on one side, and some on the other. Presently the noise of footsteps were heard approaching them. In a few moments an old Indian made his appearance, with a gun resting carelessly on his shoulder, and a young squaw following him, each of whom had a basket. As soon as they reached a point in the path between the men, Church and his company suddenly rose from their ambush, and seized them.

To prevent all collusion between them, and by the correspondence of their answers to detect the truthfulness of their statements, he examined them apart. Taking the girl one side he asked, —

"What company did you leave last ?"

"Captain Annawon's," she answered.

"How many men were with him when you left ?"

"Fifty or sixty," was her reply.

"How many miles is it to the place where you left him ?"

"I don't know miles; but he is in Squannaconk Swamp." This was in the east part of Rehoboth, near Old Taunton.

Turning from the girl, he commenced an examination of the old man. He gave precisely the same information.

"Can you get there by night?" asked Church.

"If we set out immediately, and travel fast, we may reach there by sunset."

"Who are you, and where were you going?" asked Church.

"I am one of Annawon's men, and he has sent me after some of the tribe who have gone to Mount Hope Neck to kill provision."

Church informed him that those men had been taken prisoners.

The Indian, who had gone after his father, now returned with him, bringing also another man.

The active mind of Church soon devised a plan of procedure.

"Men," said he, "will you go with me and give Annawon a visit?"

"Yes," was their unanimous answer. At the same time they told him that they knew that Annawon was a bold chieftain, and the men with him were among the bravest of the army. They doubted whether such a mere handful as they were could make any impression upon such a number of such men. Church, however, was undaunted. He said he had been a long time searching for Annawon in vain, and he had not the least doubt that Providence would protect them. Courage is sympathetic. When the men saw the fearlessness of Church, their objections became inoperative, and they desired to be led forward.

Church now said to the old man whom he had taken, —

"Will you be our pilot to Annawon?"

"You have spared my life: I am bound to serve you," was his answer.

They now set out towards Annawon's hiding-place, guided by the old man. After travelling as rapidly as possible, through woods, swamps, and thickets, for several hours, the old man suddenly halted.

"What 's the matter? have you made a discovery?" asked Church.

"No," replied the guide; "but about this hour every day Annawon sends out his scouts to see that no enemy is in sight. As soon as it begins to grow dark, they will return, and then we can move on securely." When the shades of evening were sufficiently deep to furnish them a veil of safety, they renewed their march. As they started, Church asked the old man, —

"Will you take a gun, and fight for me?"

The Indian made a low bow, and said he hoped that they would not impose such a task upon him as to fight against Captain Annawon, his old friend. "But I will go along with you, and help you, and will lay hands on any man that shall offer to hurt you."

After walking a short distance, a noise was heard. Church ordered the men to stop and listen. It was some one pounding corn. They now knew they were very near Annawon's retreat, and great caution was necessary to avoid detection. Near by was a high rock, one side of which was a perpendicular precipice; the other side formed a gentle inclined plane. Church, and two of his Indians, crept slowly and silently up the sloping side of this rock till they reached its lofty summit. They then beheld a sight which was enough to have made any other than hearts of the bravest character quail with fear. Annawon's whole band of fifty or sixty Indians were before them. By the light of their numerous fires, which illumined the surrounding darkness, they saw that they were divided into three companies. Around the fires were groups of men and women, waiting for the pots to boil, or the meat to roast, which they were engaged in cooking. At the base of the rock was Annawon's lodging-place. It was formed by a tree leaning against a rock, and sheltered on each side with bushes. Annawon, with his son, and some

CAPTURE OF ANNAWON BY STRATAGEM.

of his principal men, were there. As there was no possibility of lowering himself down the steep declivity, without detection, he crawled cautiously back and inquired of his old guide if there was no other way of entering among them. The guide told him no. All the other sides of the swamp were guarded, and the Indians themselves had been ordered to come this way; that if any attempted to enter at any other point, they would be taken for enemies, and shot. Church noticed that the men who were immediately around Annawon were not in possession of their arms. Their guns were leaning against a horizontal pole, which was supported by two crotchets, and were covered with mats to protect them from the dew. This was more favorable for him. Yet what could he do? He had only a half dozen men, and Annawon had about sixty. To attempt their capture against such odds, must have seemed like a forlorn hope. Yet Church resolved to attempt it by stratagem. He told the guide and the young woman to take their baskets on their backs, and pass into the encampment at the usual place of entrance. In this way he thought Annawon would be deceived, and would imagine it some of his own party, especially when he should recognize the old man whom he had sent after the Indians. Church crept down immediately behind the guide, with hatchet in hand, concealed by the dark shadow of his basket, which the fires caused: then came the girl with her basket, in the shadow of which crouched the rest of the party. In an instant they leaped over the head of young Annawon, who rolled his blanket around him and curled into a heap; they then sprung for the stacked guns. Old Annawon started up, and with a cry of surprise signified that he was taken. Church told him that resistance was in vain, as the swamp was invested with a large army of the English, who would kill every one who showed a disposition to fight; but if they would yield quietly, no harm should befall them. The Indians with Church, who were well known to Annawon's men, ran in among the three different divisions of the enemy, told them the same story, and exhorted them to give up their arms without resistance, or death would be the consequence of refusal, as they were surrounded by large numbers of the English. Believing the stories to be true, they passively yielded themselves prisoners of war, and delivered up all guns, hatchets, and other weapons. Having succeeded thus far, Church knew it would not do to show the least degree of timidity, as that would expose his stratagem, and death would inevitably follow. He therefore kept on a bold front, and said to Annawon, "What have you got for supper, as I intend to sup with you?"

"Taubut," answered the chief; and then turning to his women, he told them to furnish Captain Church and his men a supper.

"Which will you have," said Annawon, "cow-beef or horse-beef?"

"Cow-beef," replied Church.

In a short time it was ready, and the men made a good meal. After supper, Church told his men, if they would watch, and let him sleep for two hours, he would keep guard the rest of the night, as he had had no sleep for thirty-six hours. They agreed to the proposal, and Church laid down to sleep. But after lying half an hour, and finding it impossible, under such circumstances, to catch even a short nap, he looked after his sentinels, and found them all enjoying

"Tired Nature's sweet restorer, balmy sleep."

Church had thrown himself down by the side of Annawon, to prevent his escape. After some time, the chief arose and walked away in the darkness. He was gone so long that Church began to suspect he had given him the slip. He therefore took all the guns, placed them near to himself, and then laid down close to young Annawon, so that no attempt upon his life could be made without perilling the young chief also. After a while, the painful suspense of Church was relieved by Annawon's return. He came with a bundle in his hand. Kneeling at the feet of Church, he said, "Great captain, you have killed Philip, and conquered his country, for I believe that I and my company are the last that war against the English; so I suppose the war is ended by your means, and therefore these things belong unto you." He then drew from his bundle a belt, nine inches broad, and seven or eight feet long, most beautifully embroidered, by having figures of beasts, birds, and flowers elaborately wrought into it, and a quantity of variegated wampum, or Indian money. Another belt, also highly embroidered, was next handed him. This was used as a head dress: from it hung two flags, which fell over and ornamented the back. Then another he drew from his bundle, decorated with a star. This was designed for the breast. All of these belts were fringed with red hair, which was obtained from the Mohawks. He next brought out "two horns of glazed powder and a red blanket." "These," said Annawon, "are the royal robes and ornaments in which Philip was accustomed to array himself on important public occasions; they are all that remains of him. As you are his conqueror, I cheerfully give them to you."

As it was impossible for either of them to sleep, in the exciting circumstances in which they were placed, they spent the remainder of the night in conversation, in which the chief narrated the great victories he had won over various tribes of Indians, when he fought under Massasoit.

To Church time seemed to fly with leaden wings.

Night wore away with extreme slowness. He was impatient for the gray dawn of the morning. He had taken a large band of Indians, and was anxious to secure them before his stratagem was discovered. When it became light, he gave orders to march. They all set out for Taunton. On the way they met Lieutenant Howland, who was left behind when Church with his few men accompanied the Indian who went in search of his father. A few words told the whole story, and filled him with amazement. They spent the night at Taunton. The next day, Church sent the great body of the Indians, under the care of Howland, to Plymouth. But Annawon and a few Indian soldiers he took with himself to Rhode Island, to his family, and from thence to Plymouth. This may be regarded as the conclusion of Philip's famous war, for after this there was no organized opposition to the English. The central power which kept the enemy together was broken, and the subsequent exploits consisted mainly in pursuing and capturing small parties of Indians, who, perhaps, refused to submit quietly, for fear they would be punished for having taken up arms against the English. Some of these closing skirmishes were full of interest. They exhibited ingenious stratagems, sleepless vigilance, and great bravery. They were attended, though on a small scale, with the prominent features of savage warfare. At the close of the war, the prisoners in the hands of the English were to be disposed of. It was a grave question, What shall be done with them? Opinions were divided. Some inclined to mercy, and others to severity. The subject was discussed both as a political and religious question, and many passages of Scripture were examined in relation to it. The most knotty point of all was, What shall be done with Annawon's son, who would be his father's successor? The court asked the opinion of the ministers. Samuel Arnold, the minister of Marshfield, and John Cotton, the minister of Plymouth, expressed the opinion, that "the children of notorious traitors, rebels and murtherers, and such as have been the principal leaders and actors in such horrid villanies, and that against a whole nation, may, *salva republica*, be adjudged to death." They referred as proof to various Scripture incidents. Increase Mather seems to have been inclined to the same sentiment. Mr. Keith, minister of Bridgewater, favored a more merciful course. The conclusion was, the young chief was sold as a slave, and shipped to Bermuda. Many others of the prisoners shared the same fate. Old Annawon, and others who had killed any of the English, were executed. Church did all in his power to prevent such injustice and cruelty; but he was overruled by a more potent influence.

CHAPTER XXII.

> "Justice is lame, as well as blind, amongst us;
> The laws, corrupted to their ends that make them,
> Serve but for instruments of some new tyranny,
> That every day starts up t' enslave us deeper." — Otway.

The Colonies affected by the Home Government. — Arrival of Andros. — Encourages Episcopacy. — Declares Land Titles invalid. — Appropriates public Property to private Uses. — Prohibits Town Meetings. — Other Oppressions. — Andros imprisoned. — Nathaniel Clark seized. — Clark's Island. — The first Sabbath. — Wiswall imprisoned. — Absence from Town Meetings fined. — A Price for Wolves' Heads. — The first Selectmen. — The first Marriage. — An honored Lady. — Introduction of Neat Cattle. — First Record of Horses. — A Present to Philip. — Merry Mount. — Weetamore beheaded. — Its Effect on the Indians. — French Vessel wrecked. — The Crew seized as Prisoners. — Doctor Le Baron. — His Settlement and Marriage. — His Attachment to the Cross. — A Premium for Rats' Heads. — First public Celebration of "The Landing." — The Dinner. — The famous Rock. — Its Locality proved. — The Evidence of Elder Faunce and others. — The Rock splits. — A good Omen. — Is removed. — Treatment of Tories. — Wonderful Egg. — Dreadful Shipwreck. — Statistics.

As the colonies increased in size and importance, they attracted more of the attention of the king and parliament of Great Britain. Their condition was materially affected by the changes in the home government. What they feared most was, that attempts would be made to abridge their liberties. These apprehensions were fully realized, when, on the 29th of December, 1686, Sir Edmund Andros arrived, bringing with him the commission of governor of all the New England colonies. He was a man of arbitrary spirit, and though, at first, he made professions of liberality, he ruled like a tyrant. He abridged the freedom of the press. He encouraged episcopacy, which had never existed in Massachusetts Bay. He desired the Puritans to relinquish one of their meeting-houses for the episcopal church. Their answer was, "We cannot, with a good conscience, consent." They were compelled to yield; and by an act of tyranny, the Book of Common Prayer was read by one in a white surplice, in a Puritan place of worship, in Boston.

Those who refused to lay their hands on the Bible, when they took an oath, were fined and imprisoned. He declared the usual legal titles to lands invalid, and subjected the people to great expense to get their titles confirmed. He appropriated public and private property to the use of his own partisans. He, with his council, who were appointed by the crown, assessed all taxes. He prohibited all town meetings, except for the choice of town officers; fined and imprisoned those who spoke too freely against his administration; punished town clerks who refused to give up, at his demand, their town records. He demanded exorbitant fees for all public business; required all under his government to transact probate business in the probate court at Boston. This, of course, subjected those who resided in the distant colonies to great inconvenience, loss of time, and expense. In various other ways did he oppress the people, until they were obliged to present their complaints against him to the king. These were received with no favor. His despotic administration continued until the accession of William and Mary, when the people of the colonies rose in arms, seized Andros, confined him in prison, obliged him to resign, and then re-chose their old governor, Simon Bradstreet, who was nearly ninety years of age.

As soon as the news of the change in the government reached Plymouth, the people there laid hands upon one Nathaniel Clark, a man of similar political sentiments and spirit with Andros, whose parasite he was, and imprisoned him. One reason for this was, that Clark, under the usurped authority of Andros, had taken possession of an island in Plymouth Harbor, which had been appropriated by the town for the support of their poor.

It was the island on which the Puritans kept their first Christian Sabbath in New England, when they were in search along the coast for a harbor. It was therefore associated in their minds with pleasant, sacred reminiscences. No other spot, probably, could have been wrested from them which would have given them more pain to part with than this. So indignant were Mr. Faunce and Rev. Mr. Wiswall, the minister of Duxbury, at this high-handed robbery, that they interfered in the matter. For this interference they were prosecuted, fined, and put under bonds to appear at the higher court in Boston. Mr. Wiswall was subsequently sent to prison. As the natural result of Clark's oppressive and rapacious conduct, the people of Plymouth were incensed against him, and gladly availed themselves of the first favorable opportunity to bring him to justice.

We propose now to group together a variety of facts, having no connection with each other, yet too interesting to be omitted.

In 1646, it having been observed that town meetings were not well attended, an order was passed that every person who should be absent from such meeting after being regularly summoned, should be fined twelve pence, unless he could furnish a satisfactory excuse.

Three years afterwards, a town meeting was held at the *house* of Governor Bradford, where it was ordered that whoever should kill one or more wolves, and show the skins or heads as evidence of such death, should receive fifteen shillings for each one destroyed within the liberties of the town. On the same occasion, a number of individuals agreed "to pay two cents apiece to any Indian who shall kill a wolf, and make it known to the governor by undoubted testimony; and such as shall kill lesser wolves, shall have an axe or hatchet for each one killed." It was also agreed, that five wolf-traps should be made by several companies of the townsmen, the names of whom were to be put upon paper, that arrangements might be made to have the traps properly tended.

The first appointment of selectmen to manage the affairs of the town occurred the same year, when seven "discreet men" were chosen, whose duty it was to dispose of lands, to provide employment and support for the poor, and take charge of the affairs of the town generally. A few years after this, their powers were considerably enlarged.

The first marriage in the colony was solemnized on May 12, 1621, between Mr. Edward Winslow and Mrs. Susannah White. Mr. W. had been a widower between two and three months. The lady was the widow of Mr. William White, and mother of Peregrine White, the first English child born in the colony. Mr. Baylies says, "It is a singular coincidence, that Mrs. White should have been the first mother and the first bride in a country which has produced a race so distinguished as the New Englanders. This would have been cited by the ancients as an instance of rare and happy fortune, if we add to that the peculiar happiness of having been the wife of a distinguished governor of her own colony, and the mother of another, equally distinguished, who, to his other, added the high and solitary honor of having been the commander-in-chief of the forces of the confederate colonies, in a war involving their existence." The fortune of such a lady must be regarded as "transcendently prosperous." When Winslow was sent to England as agent for the colony in 1623, he brought back, on his return, three heifers and a bull. These were the first neat cattle introduced into the colony.

About twenty years after this, we find horses are spoken of. The first record concerning them was made in 1644, when we learn that a mare, belonging to the estate of Stephen Hopkins, was valued at six pounds sterling. Three years subsequent, a colt was appraised at four pounds sterling, and a mare and colt at fourteen pounds sterling. Ten years later, the court passed an act, that every freeholder who should own three mares, and who would "keep one horse for military service, should be freed from all military service, training, and watching." During the time that the colony was without horses, it was not an unusual thing for them to ride upon bulls, as we have seen in the case of Mr. John Alden, who went after his bride and brought her home in that manner. In 1665, the court presented Philip, the

Indian chief, with a horse. "It would gratify curiosity to know in what manner King Philip, and the natives in general, were affected by the first sight of horses and cows. Their minds must have been overwhelmed with astonishment to see men riding on horses and bulls."

There is in Quincy a beautiful swell of land near the water, about one hundred feet high, from which a fine view may be obtained of a delightful landscape, embracing on one side hill and dale, dense forest and open plain; and on the other, the numerous islands and forts in the bay, which, when the ocean is calm, appear like jewels on the surface of a mirror; whilst farther beyond may be seen the city of Boston, crowned with its elevated State House, the tall granite monument on Bunker Hill, and the white spires of numerous churches in the surrounding villages. All combined, they present, especially in a pleasant day, a scene of enchantment which, when once beheld, will not be soon forgotten. But, like many other beautiful spots of earth, it has been the scene of lawless merriment, drunken carousals, and midnight orgies. In 1625, Captain Wollaston, with thirty others, commenced a settlement here, which gave to the place the name of Mount Wollaston. Among the company was one Thomas Morton, who, when Wollaston left, managed to obtain the control of affairs. He opened trade with the natives, and devoted the profits of it to sports by day, and drunken carousals by night. He changed the name of the place to one which he doubtless designed to be more appropriate, calling it Merry Mount, where, according to the New England Memorial, they set up a "May-pole, drinking and dancing about it, and frisking about it like so many fairies, or furies rather; yea, and worse practices, as if they had anew revived and celebrated the feast of the Roman goddess Flora, or the beastly practices of the mad bacchanalians." He furnished the Indians with gunpowder, and taught them how to use it. He supplied them with ardent spirits. He gave servants their liberty, and, being destitute of moral principle, he encouraged all kinds of dissipation. The government at Plymouth at first wrote to him admonitory letters. To these he gave no heed; until, finally, his influence becoming so deleterious, they sent Captain Standish to seize him. When Standish arrived, he found Morton prepared to resist him; but by adopting, as he well knew how, timely and decisive measures, he succeeded in seizing him and carrying him to Plymouth. Morton was sent to England, but was permitted to return the following year. He indulged in various accusations and bitter invectives against the Puritans, which, after his return, were used as evidence against him. He was denominated the accuser of the brethren. He was tried by the court, who fined him one hundred pounds. Being destitute of property, he was unable to pay it. It is said that nothing but his old age saved him from the whipping-post. He withdrew to Acamenticus, where he terminated his dissolute course a year or two after.

The old-fashioned method of lining the hymns, which is still practised in some parts of the country, was introduced into the Plymouth church in 1681. One line was read, and after this was sung then another was read, and so on to the end of the hymn. It is said that this practice was proposed in the church by a brother *who could not read.* The pastor first announced the number of the psalm, and then the elder lined it off.

In the month of August, 1667, Weetamore, the squaw sachem of Pocasset, was drowned in attempting to escape from her pursuers, by crossing Tetticut River on a frail raft. Some of the inhabitants of Taunton, finding the dead body of a squaw in Mettapoisett, cut off her head. It was found to be the unfortunate Weetamore. She had been bitterly opposed to the English, and, according to Doctor Mather's testimony, "she was next unto Philip, in respect of the mischief that hath been done." When her head was placed upon a pole in Taunton, the Indian prisoners who were there instantly recognized it, and "made a most horrid and diabolical lamentation, crying out that it was their queen's head."

It is painful to contemplate such unnecessary barbarity. It is an illustration of the tendencies of war to blunt and harden the sensibilities of the heart.

In 1696, a vessel was wrecked in Buzzard's Bay. It proved to be a French privateer. The crew were seized and carried as prisoners to Boston. This was after the colonial charter of Plymouth was abrogated, and she was united with the colony of Massachusetts Bay, as a British province. It was for this reason that they were taken to Boston, instead of Plymouth. Among these shipwrecked prisoners was a surgeon by the name of Le Baron. As Plymouth was at that time destitute of a physician, Dr. Le Baron was called upon to perform a surgical operation there. He did this with so much success, that the selectmen of the town sent a petition to Lieutenant Governor Stoughton, praying for Le Baron's liberation, in order that he might settle as a physician in Plymouth. Their petition being granted, the imprisoned Le Baron took up his abode among them, and entered upon his professional career. He formed an acquaintance with Mary Wilder, to whom he was soon after united in marriage. He continued the practice of medicine here until his death, which occurred in 1704. Le Baron was a rigid Catholic. So strong were his religious prepossessions, that he never went to sleep at night without placing a small cross on his breast. He was a man of benevolent disposition, of which we have one evidence in a donation which he made of fifty acres of woodland to the town. It is stated by Thatcher, that "from this stock all that bear the name of Le Baron in this country are descended, and they are numerous and respectable." This, of course, is true only upon the supposition that no others of the same name have ever immigrated to America since his day.

In 1738, it was voted, that for every full-grown rat that should be killed, threepence should be paid out of the public treasury; and six years later it was voted, that every male head of a family should procure ten grown rats' heads, or pay a fine of sixpence per head for all that fell short.

The first time that the landing of the Pilgrim fathers was publicly celebrated in Plymouth was December 22, 1769. The Old Colony Club, which had been formed in January of the same year, originated and carried through the celebration. The morning was opened with a discharge of cannon. An elegant silk flag waved in the breeze from the top of the hall, bearing the inscription, "Old Colony, 1620." At 11, A. M., the members of the club assembled in the hall, and from thence proceeded to an inn kept by Mr. Howland, upon the identical spot where stood the first licensed house of the old colony. As some may be interested to know the kind of fare with which they were furnished on that occasion, we will give the dishes. "1, a large baked Indian whortleberry pudding; 2, a dish of sauquetach, (pronounced sukketash, corn and beans boiled together;) 3, a dish of clams; 4, a dish of oysters and a dish of codfish; 5, a haunch of venison, roasted in the first jack brought to the colony; 6, a dish of sea-fowl; 7, a dish of frost fish and eels; 8, an apple pie; 9, a course of cranberry tarts, and cheese made in the Old Colony." In imitation of their ancestors, all luxury and extravagance were avoided, the dishes being dressed in the plainest manner. After dinner, a procession was formed of the members, headed by the steward of the club bearing a large volume of the laws of the colony, who marched hand in hand to the hall. When they arrived in front of the hall, a company of the descendants of the first settlers formed a regular file, and greeted them with a discharge of small arms and three cheers. These were returned by the club, and "the gentlemen generously treated." After this, the scholars of the grammar school joined in singing a song appropriate to the occasion. At sunset, a cannon was fired and the flag struck. In the evening the hall was beautifully illuminated. The president occupied the antique chair, which was formerly the property of Governor Bradford. Addresses were made, sentiments expressed, and toasts drank. At 11, P. M., a cannon was fired, and after three hearty cheers the company withdrew.

The thrilling emotions awakened in the mind by a visit to the famous Forefathers' Rock, are sometimes checked by the thought that perhaps there is some uncertainty in its traditionary location. It becomes, therefore, an interesting question, On what evidence does the generally received opinion rest, that this is the identical rock on which the Pilgrims first stepped? In answer to this question, Mr. Russell, in his interesting "Guide to Plymouth," says, "Besides the general and undisputed tradition which designates it as that on which the fathers landed, it was ascertained to be the same on an interesting occasion in the life of Elder Thomas Faunce, the last ruling elder in the first church of Plymouth, who was born in the year 1646, and died in the year 1745, at the advanced age of ninety-nine years. In the year 1741, the elder, upon learning that a wharf was about to be built near, or over the rock which, up to that period, had kept its undisturbed rights at the water's edge, and fearing that the march of improvement might subject it to injury, expressed much uneasiness. Though residing three miles from the village of Plymouth, and then in declining health, he left home, and, in the presence of many citizens, pointed out the rock we have described as being that on which the Pilgrims, with whom he was contemporary and well acquainted, had uniformly declared to be the same on which they landed in 1620. Upon this occasion, this venerable and excellent man took a final leave of this cherished memorial of the fathers. The circumstances above related were frequently mentioned by the late Hon. Ephraim Spooner, deceased, who was present upon the occasion connected with Elder Faunce. He was deacon of the church of Plymouth forty-one years, and fifty-two years town clerk, and died March, 1818, aged eighty-three years. The same information was communicated by Mrs. Joanna White, widow of Gideon White, deceased, who was intimately acquainted in the family of Elder Faunce. She died in 1810, aged ninety-five years. And the same account has been transmitted by other aged persons, now deceased, within the recollection of many now living."

During the political excitements that preceded the declaration of independence, the inhabitants of Plymouth were not idle. They were deeply interested in the questions of the day, and adopted efficient methods of exhibiting their opposition to the tyrannical measures of the British Parliament. In 1772, a town meeting was called, at which a petition, signed by over a hundred inhabitants, was presented, calling attention to the distressed and alarming situation of the country, in consequence of the oppressive policy of the British government, and praying the town to take the subject into careful considera- tion. After this petition was read, the town appointed a standing committee, to open a correspondence with other towns upon the existing troubles, and the best course to pursue with regard to them, and to adopt any other measures which, in their judgment, the exigency of the case might demand. As the unjust and tyrannical laws of the English Parliament increased, the opposition of the Plymouthites was strengthened.

In 1774, it was resolved to use the famous Forefathers' Rock, as fuel to increase in intensity the flame of indignation, already burning, against the tyranny of the mother country.

For this purpose, it was deemed desirable that the rock should be raised from its natural bed and placed in a central part of the town, where it might be daily and hourly seen, and where it might be constantly, though silently, saying, —

"Come listen to my story,
  Though often told before,
Of men who passed to glory,
  Through toil and travail sore;
Of men who did for conscience' sake
  Their native land forego,
And sought a home and FREEDOM here,
  Two hundred years ago."

A large number of the patriotic citizens of the town assembled on the interesting occasion. Forty oxen were brought down to the shore to draw the rock from its ancient, secluded resting-place into its more exposed position. By means of powerful screws it was raised from its bed; but in the attempt to place it upon the carriage, it fell apart. As no fracture had been discovered in it, and as it separated without violence, it excited great surprise. This singular phenomenon was at once seized upon by the enthusiastic patriots of the town as a most favorable omen. They explained it as significant of a division of the British empire. After deliberation, it was decided to remove only one part of the rock. This, after being placed upon the car, was slowly drawn through the streets, followed by a great number of persons, to the Liberty Pole Square, near the meeting-house, where it is said a flag was raised over it, containing the brief, stern motto of defiance, "Liberty or Death."

Having accomplished its object there, it made another journey on July 4, 1834, to its present location, in front of Pilgrim Hall. This was another great day for Plymouth. The whole town was alive and full of excitement. Old and young, males and females, were inspired by the occasion. The children of the several schools in the town, both boys and girls, headed the procession. They had with them a car bearing a model of the Mayflower, beautifully decorated. It was drawn by six boys. After them came the older inhabitants, and others, many of whom were the lineal descendants of the Pilgrims, and bore their names. They passed over that elevation of land known as Cole's Hill, where the remains of those who died during the first winter were laid. When they arrived in front of Pilgrim Hall, and deposited the precious memorial in what is presumed to be its last resting-place, a volley of musketry was fired over it by the Standish Guards; an address was delivered by Dr. Charles Cotton, and devotional services were conducted by Rev. Dr. Kendall. This portion of the rock is now protected by a noble structure, serving the double purpose of security to the rock, and a monument to the Pilgrims. Thatcher's description of it is as follows: "The fabric was erected in June, 1835, and consists of a perfect ellipse, forty-one feet in perimeter, formed of wrought-iron bars, five feet high, resting on a base of hammered granite. The heads of the perpendicular bars are harpoons and boat hooks, arranged alternately. The whole is embellished with emblematic figures of cast iron. The base of the railing is studded with emblems of marine shells, placed alternately reversed, having a striking effect. The upper part of the railing is encircled with a wreath of iron castings, in imitation of heraldry curtains, fringed with festoons; of these are forty-one, bearing the names in bas-relief of the forty-one Puritan fathers who signed the memorable compact, while in the cabin of the Mayflower, at Cape Cod, 1620. This valuable and interesting acquisition reflects honor on all who have taken an interest in the undertaking. In the original design, by George W. Brimmer, Esq., ingenuity and correct taste are displayed; and in all its parts, the work is executed with much judgment and skill. The castings are executed in the most approved style of art. This appropriate memorial will last for ages, and the names and story of the great founders of our nation will be made familiar to the latest generation."

Fragments of this rock are scattered far and wide throughout our country. That intelligent Frenchman, and careful observer of the spirit and institutions of the Americans, De Tocqueville, says, "This rock has become an object of veneration in the United States. I have seen bits of it carefully preserved in several towns of the Union. Does not this sufficiently show that all human power and greatness is in the soul of man? Here is a stone which the feet of a few outcasts pressed for an instant, and the stone becomes famous; it is treasured by a great nation; its very dust is shared as a relic. And what has become of the gateways of a thousand palaces? Who cares for them?"

During the struggle that preceded the independence of the United States, there were in Plymouth two parties, the whigs and tories, the former of whom were by far the most numerous. The tories sympathized with the king and Parliament, and were, therefore, considered as enemies to America. They were subjected to various insults and punishments. The public authority obliged them to make a full and public recantation of their unpopular political opinions over their own signatures. These were published in the papers. When summary punishment was inflicted upon any of them by the populace, different methods were adopted. Sometimes the lawless rioters would amuse themselves with a sport which they called "smoking the tories." This was done by confining the offenders in a room, building a fire on the hearth, and then covering the top of the chimney. Of course, all the smoke would be retained in the room. At other times they would apply a coat of tar to the person, and cover it with feathers. Not unfrequently they would make the poor horse of some obstinate tory suffer for the sins of his master, by shaving his tail, and cropping his ears. On one occasion, a man by the name of Dunbar exposed for sale in the market a beef ox, which had been killed by a tory, who had rendered himself peculiarly obnoxious to the citizens. As soon as this was known, a number of the more excitable portion of the populace assembled together, put Dunbar in the carcass of the ox, clothing him with it as if it were a coat; they then tied the tripe around his neck for a cravat, and in that humiliating condition carted him out of town. Being a man of determined spirit, he refused to keep out. He shortly returned on horseback. He was ordered off, but obstinately refused to go. The people being highly incensed at what they regarded as stubbornness, tied him on his horse and conducted him off. He resisted with so much energy as to be considerably injured. The crowd finally procured a cart, in which they conveyed him some distance beyond the town.

During this year, the British general, Howe, was engaged in military operations to reduce the Americans to submission. A harmless trick was resorted to in Plymouth, perhaps by a tory, by which public excitement was increased. An egg was discovered, on the shell of which could be plainly read, "O America, America! Howe shall be thy conqueror." It was taken from the nest, and exhibited to the people when assembled for public worship. So great was the agitation which it occasioned, that for some time the meeting was suspended. The tories pretended to believe it was a supernatural revelation. They construed it as an omen favorable to their cause. Some of the opposite party were also inclined to the same opinion, as they knew not how to account for it in any other way. But one less credulous than the rest gave to the matter a tinge of the ridiculous, by observing that it was absurd to suppose that the Almighty would reveal his decrees to man through the medium of an *old hen.* The affair not only became the town talk and a nine days' wonder, but was also the subject of grave newspaper comment, and the alarm which it produced in the minds of the timid and superstitious was truly surprising.

In the month of December, 1778, a catastrophe of a most appalling nature occurred off Plymouth Harbor. The brig General Arnold, carrying twenty guns, with a crew of one hundred and five souls, under the command of James Magee, of Boston, left that port on the 24th, on a cruise, this country being then engaged in war with Great Britain. Being destitute of a pilot, she was driven upon the flats near Plymouth. She soon filled with water, when the order was given to cut away the masts. As many of the men were drunk, it was difficult to keep them in a state of subordination. A tremendous storm came on, accompanied with snow and sleet. On Saturday, the 26th, a considerable number of the men died. On Sunday morning the vessel was in a fearfully perilous condition. She was completely enshrouded in ice. So violent were the wind and the raging waves, that the inhabitants on shore found it impossible to reach her, or to extend the least assistance. The horrors of their situation may be inferred from what was found to be their condition the next day. By that time the sea had so far subsided that she could be visited. "It is scarcely possible for the human mind to conceive of a more appalling spectacle. The ship was sunk ten feet in the sand. The waves had been for about thirty-six hours sweeping the main deck; the men had crowded to the quarter deck, and even here they were obliged to pile together dead bodies to make room for the living. Seventy dead bodies frozen into all imaginable postures, were strewn over the deck or attached to the shrouds and the spars; about thirty exhibited signs of life, but were unconscious whether in life or death. The bodies remained in the posture in which they died, the features dreadfully distorted; some were erect, some bending forward, some sitting with the head resting upon the knees, and some with both arms extended, clinging to spars or some parts of the vessel. The few survivors and the dead bodies were brought over the ice on sleds and boards, and the dead were piled on the floor of the court house, exhibiting a scene calculated to impress even the most callous heart with deep humility and sorrow. It has been said that the Rev. Mr. Robbins fainted when called to perform the religious solemnities. Those bodies that were to be deposited in coffins were first put into the town brook; a considerable number were seen floating on the water, fastened by ropes, that their form might be made to conform to the coffin. But about sixty were thrown into a large pit as they were taken from the vessel. This pit is in a hollow on the south-west side of the burial ground, and remains without a stone. The greater part of those who were found alive expired soon after." The captain survived. He drank no spirits, but poured it freely into his boots. Almost all those who drank liquor perished, "several being found dead in the very spot where they drank it." What a powerful argument is this in favor of total abstinence! This mournful catastrophe, without doubt, was made the subject of Sabbath discourse, and we can imagine what must have been the solemnity and impressiveness of the service.

We have not in the preceding pages given any information as to the increase of Plymouth at different periods. This omission will now be supplied. It will be remembered that one hundred came over in the Mayflower, in 1620, of whom one half died during the first winter. In 1624, there were one hundred and eighty; in 1629, three hundred. In 1631, there were between four and five hundred. In 1643, the males from sixteen to sixty years of age were one hundred and forty-six. In 1646, the number of voters, seventy-nine. Four years afterwards it was only fifty-one. In 1683, the voters numbered fifty-five, and in 1689 they amounted to seventy-five. Leaping over a century, we find in 1764 the whole number of inhabitants, including seventy-seven colored persons and forty-eight Indians, was two thousand two hundred and twenty-five. In 1776, the year of the declaration of independence, they numbered two thousand six hundred and fifty-five. In 1783, at the termination of the revolutionary war, there were only two thousand three hundred and eighty; in 1800, three thousand five hundred and twenty-four; in 1820, four thousand three hundred and forty-eight; in 1840, five thousand two hundred and eighty-one.

CHAPTER XXIII.

> "How could my tongue
> Take pleasure and be lavish in their praise?
> How could I speak their nobleness of nature,
> Their open, manly heart, their courage, constancy,
> And inborn truth, unknowing to dissemble?
> They are the men in whom my soul delights,
> In whom, next Heaven, I trust." — Rowe.

Attachment to the Scriptures. — Reason of Puritanic Singularities. — Precise in their Manners. — Their Ministers of equal Authority. — Their Government republican. — Their Self-reliance and divine Dependence. — Were not vindictive. — Did not come here to establish universal Toleration. — Their Object was Liberty for themselves. — This the Origin of their Opposition to other Sects. — The prospective Influence of their Principles.

Having now given an account of some of the most important events which have occurred in the history of Plymouth since its first settlement, we cannot, perhaps, more appropriately close the subject than with a brief sketch of the character and principles of the Puritans.

One of their most prominent traits was a conscientious adherence to what they believed were the teachings of the Sacred Scriptures. To them the authority of God was all and in all. Believing as they did that the Bible was his revealed will, they made that their exclusive guide in matters of faith and practice. Creeds, characters, and customs were all tried by this unfailing test, and all was rejected which, in their opinion, did not stand this ordeal. Laws and regulations adopted by them, which, at the present day, are stigmatized as singularities, were, in many instances, the legitimate fruits of their strict adherence to the teachings of the Bible. The peculiarities of some of their forms of legislation were occasioned by their imitation of ancient Jewish customs. Thus, in New Haven the members of the constituent committee were called the "seven pillars hewn out of the house of Wisdom," and Rhode Island performed for one or two years a "Jewish masquerade." Their language was quaint, because interlarded with the phraseology of Scripture. They disapproved of wigs, veils, and long hair. They were equally opposed to immodest and extravagant apparel, because both were alike at variance with the simplicity and purity inculcated by the Bible. They were precise in their manners, because, as one of them said, they had "a precise God to deal with." They repudiated crosses and beads, surplice and prayer books. To their minds, these were too intimately allied to Rome. They denied the superiority of the bishops over other orders of ordained ministers. With them, all the ministry occupied the same official platform—they were all bishops, possessing equal official privileges and powers. They maintained that the church was independent of the ministry; that every church possessed the right of electing its own pastor; that no power out of themselves, whether king or archbishop, had any right to impose upon them a minister, contrary to their wishes. In ecclesiastical and civil government they were republican — the majority ruled.

Although they cherished strong confidence in God, and acknowledged his hand in all the events of providence, they did not dispense with self-reliance. They were Calvinists, but not fatalists. They believed that as men have purposes, so has God; that these purposes result from his infinite wisdom and goodness, and will inevitably be accomplished, without the least interference with the free agency of man. They cultivated confidence in God in conjunction with self-dependence. Their works went with their faith, and were the fruits of it. Cromwell developed the union of these apparently conflicting principles, when, in making an attack in a rainy day, he said to his soldiers, "Trust in God and keep your powder dry;" and when on another occasion he said, "He that prays best and preaches best, will fight the best."

The Puritans were not vindictive. We know there are those who deny this, and who assert that they were governed by "a bigoted despotism, with which they domineered over all who departed from their stern creed, and who would not consent to stand day and night in the strait jacket in which they enveloped alike the feeble and the strong." We are aware that it has been said, "the tyranny with which they were oppressed in England was light in comparison to the relentless and unsated animosity with which they pursued the Quakers, the most harmless and kindest sect the world ever saw." It is not uncommon to meet with indiscriminate, wholesale denunciations of this character. From some representations which have been given, it would be easy to infer that the Puritans were a most bigoted, tyrannical, superstitious, revengeful, and persecuting sect; that their excellences have been altogether overrated, and their memories too highly honored. With all this we have no sympathy. It is our firm conviction, that the more their principles are understood and their characters known, the more they will be admired. That they had their imperfections, is not denied. That a number of their particular measures, such as their selling captured Indians into slavery, their barbarous practice of beheading, quartering, and exposing portions of the bodies of their enemies, their persecutions of the Quakers, Baptists, and others, and their cruel treatment of reputed witches, should be strongly condemned, is also admitted. These are dark shadows in their history, the existence of which cannot be too deeply regretted. But we should remember that they lived in a darker period than the present; that what public opinion now condemns, public opinion then approved; that their conduct was in harmony with the spirit of their age.

Their persecutions of the Quakers, the Baptists, and others whom they termed schismatics, seemed to them to be demanded by the necessity of the case. In respect to the Quakers, it cannot be concealed that they gave provocation. The Friends of the present generation are not guilty of the practices of those who lived two centuries ago, neither do they approve them. It has been well said, that "if the essential guilt of persecution would be aggravated when aimed against the quiet, patient philanthropist of the present day, it does not therefore follow that it would be attended with like aggravation, however wicked else, when the subject was the mischievous madman of two centuries ago, with whom the Massachusetts colonists had to deal. We suppose that the duty of toleration, comprehensive though it be, stops somewhere short of allowing men and women, for conscience' sake, to run as naked as they were born through the streets and into the churches; or, at all events, that it does not require the permitting of people to gain a name like Abraham's, by sacrificing their own sons, as one of the Quakers in 1658 was proceeding to do, when his neighbors, alarmed by the boy's cries, broke into the house in time to interfere."

To do the Puritans justice, we should examine their conduct from *their stand point;* we should look at it through their eyes and with their heart. If they had come here in order to establish a government of universal religious toleration, to provide a peaceful home for all religious sects, then their persecution of others would have been at direct variance with their principles. But this was not their object. They braved a winter's voyage across the Atlantic that they might find a place where they could worship God according to their own conscience, without *molestation from others.* They sought liberty for themselves, not for the world; a place of freedom where they could serve their Maker, and train up their children according to their own views of duty, without the embarrassment of an arbitrary government, or of *opposing sects.* When, therefore, other denominations presented themselves within their limits, and claimed the right of promulgating sentiments which the Puritans regarded as unscriptural and highly dangerous, they were prohibited. "We cannot permit it," said the Pilgrim fathers. "The diffusion of such sentiments through our little community will disturb our peace, will corrupt the purity of our faith, will engender hatred and strife, and will imperil the souls of our children. The toleration of such sects among us will defeat the object for which, with so much suffering and toil, we have come to America. If you desire liberty, go off by yourselves, and form an independent colony as we have; but come not within our borders, to be snares to our feet and thorns in our side." But when those whom they deemed heretics refused to go, they verily thought they were doing God service in punishing them, as Saul of Tarsus did, when persecuting the Christians of the first century. To form our opinion of them with the impression on our minds that they possessed all the light upon religious freedom which we enjoy, is to treat them unfairly. The great doctrine of "soul liberty" they had not received, although it was proffered them by Roger Williams, and therefore our condemnation of them must not be quite so severe as if they had embraced it.

Although these considerations do not justify the severities of the Puritans towards other sects, they are yet worthy of examination, when forming our opinion of their character. They were industrious, frugal, self-denying, and persevering; they were the friends of education, and early endowed schools and colleges. They were sympathetic, benevolent, and affectionate. They endeavored to make the will of God their rule of conduct, and the glory of God the great end of life. If their descendants are sufficiently wise to adopt similar principles, and consistently maintain them in all the relations of life, the institutions which they have planted, and which are the living fountains of our prosperity, will continue to bless our country till the end of time.

> "O, never may they rest unsung,
> While Liberty can find a tongue !
> Twine, Gratitude, a wreath for them,
> More deathless than the diadem,
> Who to life's noblest end
> Gave up life's noblest powers,
> And bade the legacy descend
> Down, down to us and ours." — SPRAGUE

CATALOGUE

OF VALUABLE WORKS PUBLISHED BY

GOULD AND LINCOLN,

NO. 59, WASHINGTON STREET,

BOSTON.

The attention of the public is invited to an examination of the merits of the works described in this Catalogue, embracing valuable contributions to General Literature, Science, and Theology.

Besides their own publications, they have a general assortment of books in the various departments of literature, and can supply every thing in their line of business on the lowest terms, wholesale and retail.

PRINCIPLES OF ZOÖLOGY; Touching the Structure, Development, Distribution, and Natural Arrangement of the RACES OF ANIMALS, living and extinct, with numerous illustrations. For the use of Schools and Colleges. Part I., COMPARATIVE PHYSIOLOGY. By LOUIS AGASSIZ and AUGUSTUS A. GOULD.

"The design of this work is to furnish an epitome of the leading principles of the science of Zoölogy, as deduced from the present state of knowledge, so illustrated as to be intelligible to the beginning student. No similar treatise now exists in this country, and indeed, some of the topics have not been touched upon in the language, unless in a strictly technical form, and in scattered articles."

"Being designed for American students, the illustrations have been drawn, as far as possible, from American objects. * * * Popular names have been employed as far as possible, and to the scientific names an English termination has generally been given. The first part is devoted to Comparative Physiology, as the basis of Classification; the second, to Systematic Zoölogy, in which the principles of Classification will be applied, and the principal groups of animals briefly characterized." — *Extracts from the Preface.*

MODERN FRENCH LITERATURE; By L. RAYMOND DE VÉRICOUR, formerly lecturer in the Royal Athenæum of Paris, member of the Institute of France, &c. American edition, brought down to the present day, and revised with notes by WILLIAM S. CHASE. With a fine portrait of LAMARTINE.

*** This Treatise has received the highest praise as a comprehensive and thorough survey of the various departments of Modern French Literature. It contains biographical and critical notes of all the prominent names in Philosophy, Criticism, History, Romance, Poetry, and the Drama; and presents a full and impartial consideration of the Political Tendencies of France, as they may be traced in the writings of authors equally conspicuous as Scholars and as Statesmen. Mr. Chase, who has been the Parisian correspondent of several leading periodicals of this country, is well qualified, from a prolonged residence in France, his familiarity with its Literature, and by a personal acquaintance with many of these authors, to introduce the work of De Véricour to the American public.

"This is the only complete treatise of the kind on this subject, either in French or English, and has received the highest commendation. Mr. Chase is well qualified to introduce the work to the public. The book cannot fail to be both useful and popular." — *New York Evening Post.*

RELIGIOUS PROGRESS;

DISCOURSES ON THE DEVELOPMENT OF THE CHRISTIAN CHARACTER.

BY WILLIAM R. WILLIAMS, D. D.

12*mo., Cloth; price,* 85 *Cents.*

From H. J. Ripley, D. D., Prof of Sacred Rhetoric, &c., Newton Theol. Inst.

Strong conceptions, suggested by earnest conviction, arrest the reader's attention in this volume, no less than the author's characteristic beauty of thought and language. Historical and other illustrations of sentiments are apt and abundant; every page almost betraying the wide comprehension of knowledge which distinguishes the author. These Discourses cannot fail to make the heart better, while they inform the understanding and gratify a cultivated taste.

"This book is a rare phenomenon in these days. It is a rich exposition of Scripture, with a fund of practical, religious wisdom, conveyed in a style so strong and so massive, as to remind one of the English writers of two centuries ago; and yet it abounds in fresh illustrations drawn from every — even the latest opened — field of science and of literature." — *Methodist Quarterly.*

"His power of apt and forcible illustration is almost without a parallel among recent writers. The mute page springs into life beneath the magic of his radiant imagination. But this is never at the expense of solidity of thought or strength of argument. It is seldom indeed that a mind of so much poetical invention yields such a willing homage to the logical element. He employs his brilliant fancies for the elucidation and ornament of truth, but never for its discovery." — *Harpers' Monthly Miscellany.*

"With warm and glowing language, Dr. Williams exhibits and enforces this truth, every page radiant with 'thoughts that burn,' and leave their indelible impression upon the candid and intelligent mind." — *N. Y. Com. Advertiser.*

"The strength and compactness of argumentation, the correctness and beauty of style, and the importance of the animating idea of the discourses, are worthy of the high reputation of Dr. Williams, and place them among the most finished homiletic productions of the day. We could wish their judicious thoughts and animated periods might secure the study of every Christian." — *N. Y. Evangelist.*

"This work is from the pen of one of the brightest lights of the American pulpit. We scarcely know of any living writer who has a finer command of powerful thought and glowing, impressive language, than he. The present volume will advance, if possible, the reputation which his previous works have acquired for him." — *Albany Evening Atlas.*

"Dr. Williams has no superior among American divines, in profound and exact learning, and brilliancy of style. He seems familiar with the literature of the world, and lays his vast resources under contribution to illustrate and adorn every theme which he investigates. We wish the volume could be placed in every religious family in the country." — *Phila. Chr. Chronicle.*

We venture to predict that this work will take its place at once among the classics of American literature." — *N. Y. Recorder.*

"These sermons are certainly able and eloquent productions; a valuable contribution to those efforts which are making, in various directions, to prevent the self-sufficiency of the nineteenth century from forgetting its allegiance to God and his Christ, and to wake up the true church to the duty, even as it has the power, to extend over the world its spiritual government." — *N. Y. Chr. Inquirer.*

THE WORKS OF JOHN HARRIS, D D.

THE PRE-ADAMITE EARTH: Contributions to Theological Science. 12mo. Price 85 cents.

"It is a book for thinking men." It opens new trains of thought to the reader — puts him in a new position to survey the wonders of God's works; and compels Natural Science to bear her decided testimony in support of Divine Truth." — *Philadelphia Ch. Observer.*

MAN PRIMEVAL; Or, the Constitution and Primitive Condition of the Human Being. A Contribution to Theological Science. With a finely engraved portrait of the author; 12mo. cloth, price $1.25.

*** This is the second volume of a series of works on Theological Science. The first was received with much favor — the present is a continuation of the principles which were seen holding their way through the successive kingdoms of primeval nature, and are here resumed and exhibited in their next higher application to individual man.

"His copious and beautiful illustrations of the successive laws of the Divine Manifestation, have yielded us inexpressible delight." — *Lond. Eclectic Review.*

THE GREAT COMMISSION; Or, the Christian Church constituted and charged to convey the Gospel to the World. A Prize Essay. With an Introductory Essay, by W. R. WILLIAMS, D.D. Sixth thousand. 12mo. Price $1.00.

"Of the several productions of Dr. Harris,—all of them of great value,—that now before us is destined, probably, to exert the most powerful influence in forming the religious and missionary character of the coming generations. But the vast fund of argument and instruction comprised in these pages will excite the admiration and inspire the gratitude of thousands in our own land as well as in Europe. Every clergyman and pious and reflecting layman ought to possess the volume, and make it familiar by repeated perusal."—*Boston Recorder.*

THE GREAT TEACHER; Or, Characteristics of our Lord's Ministry. With an Introductory Essay, by H. HUMPHREY, D.D. Tenth thousand. 12mo. Price 85 cents.

"The book itself must have cost much meditation, much communion on the bosom of Jesus, and much prayer. Its style is, like the country which gave it birth, beautiful, varied, finished, and everywhere delightful. But the style of this work is its smallest excellence. It will be read: it ought to be read. It will find its way to many parlors, and add to the comforts of many a happy fireside. The reader will rise from each chapter, not able, perhaps, to carry with him many striking remarks or apparent paradoxes, but he will have a sweet impression made upon his soul, like that which soft and touching music makes when every thing about it is appropriate. The writer pours forth a clear and beautiful light, like that of the evening lighthouse, when it sheds its rays upon the sleeping waters, and covers them with a surface of gold. We can have no sympathy with a heart which yields not to impressions delicate and holy, which the perusal of this work will naturally make." — *Hampshire Gazette.*

MISCELLANIES; Consisting principally of Sermons and Essays. With an introductory Essay and notes, by J. BELCHER, D.D. 16mo. Price 75 cents.

"Some of these essays are among the finest in the language; and the warmth and energy of religious feeling manifested, render them peculiarly the treasure of the closet and the Christian fireside." — *Bangor Gazette.*

MAMMON; Or, Covetousness, the Sin of the Christian Church. A Prize Essay. 18mo. Price 45 cents. Twentieth thousand.

ZEBULON; Or, the Moral Claims of Seamen stated and enforced. 18mo. Price 25 cents.

THE ACTIVE CHRISTIAN; Containing "The Witnessing Church," etc. 32mo. Price 31 cents.

CHURCH HISTORY.—POLITY AND MEMBERSHIP.

THE APOSTOLICAL AND PRIMITIVE CHURCH; Popular in its government and simple in its worship. By LYMAN COLEMAN. With an introductory essay, by Dr. AUGUSTUS NEANDER, of Berlin. Second Edit. 12mo. cloth. Price $1.25.

From the Professors in Andover Theological Seminary.

"The undersigned are pleased to hear that you are soon to publish a new edition of the 'Primitive Church,' by LYMAN COLEMAN. They regard this volume as the result of extensive and original research; as embodying very important materials for reference, much sound thought and conclusive argument. In their estimation, it may both interest and instruct the intelligent layman, may be profitably used as a Text Book for Theological Students, and should especially form a part of the libraries of clergymen. The introduction, by NEANDER, is of itself sufficient to recommend the volume to the literary public." LEONARD WOODS, BELA B. EDWARDS, RALPH EMERSON, EDWARD A. PARK.

THE CHURCH MEMBER'S HAND BOOK. A Guide to the Doctrines and Practices of Baptist Churches. By Rev. WILLIAM CROWELL. 18mo. Cloth. Price 37½ cents.

"We have never met with a book of this size that contained so full and complete a synopsis of the Doctrines and Practice of the Baptist, or any other church, as this. Mr. Crowell is one of the ablest writers in the denomination, and if there is a subject in the whole range of Christianity which he is pre-eminently qualified to discuss, it is the one before us. The 'Hand Book' is not an abridgment of the 'Church Member's Manual,' by the same author, but is written expressly as a brief, plain guide to young members of the church. It appears to have been prepared with much care and labor, and is just such a book as is needed by every young church member; we might safely add, and by most of the older members in the denomination; for there is a vast amount of information in it that will be found of practical use to all."—*Christian Secretary.*

"It is concise, clear, and comprehensive; and, as an exposition of ecclesiastical principles and practice, is worthy of careful study of all the young members of our churches. We hope it may be widely circulated, and that the youthful thousands of our Israel may become familiar with its pages."—*Watchman and Reflector.*

THE CHURCH IN EARNEST; By JOHN ANGELL JAMES. 18mo. cloth; price 50 cents.

"A very seasonable publication. The church universal needs a re-awakening to its high vocation, and this is a book to effect, so far as human intellect can, the much desired resuscitation."—*N. Y. Com. Adv.*

"We are glad to see that this subject has arrested the pen of Mr. James. We welcome and commend it. Let it be scattered like autumn leaves. We believe its perusal will do much to impress a conviction of the high mission of the Christian, and much to arouse the Christian to fulfil it."—*N. Y. Recorder.*

"We rejoice that this work has been republished in this country, and we cannot too strongly commend it to the serious perusal of the churches of every name."—*Christian Alliance.*

"Mr. James's writings all have one object, to do execution. He writes under the impulse—Do something, do it. He studies not to be a profound or learned, but a practical writer. He aims to raise the standard of piety, holiness in the heart, and holiness of life. The influence which this work will exert on the church must be highly salutary."—*Boston Recorder.*

THE CHURCH MEMBER'S GUIDE, By Rev. J. A. JAMES. Edited by Rev. J. O. CHOULES. New Edition; with an Introductory Essay, by Rev. H. WINSLOW. 18mo. cloth. Price 38 cents.

A pastor writes—"I sincerely wish that every professor of religion in the land may possess this excellent manual. I am anxious that every member of my church should possess it, and shall be happy to promote its circulation still more extensively."

"The spontaneous effusion of our heart, on laying the book down, was,—may every church-member in our land soon possess this book, and be blessed with all the happiness which conformity to its evangelic sentiments and directions is calculated to confer."—*Christian Secretary.*

THE EXTENT OF THE ATONEMENT, in its relation to God and the Universe. By THOMAS W. JENKYN, D.D. 12mo. cloth. Price 85 cents.

"We have examined this work with profound interest and become deeply impressed with its value. Its style is lucid, its analysis perfect, its spirit and tendencies eminently evangelical. We have nowhere else seen the atonement so clearly defined, or vindicated on grounds so appreciable." *New York Recorder.*

"As a treatise on the grand relation of the Atonement, it is a book which may be emphatically said to contain the 'seeds of things,' the elements of mightier and nobler contributions of thought respecting the sacrifice of Christ, than any modern production. It is characterized by highly original and dense trains of thought, which make the reader feel that he is holding communion with a mind that can 'mingle with the universe.' We consider this volume as setting the long and fiercely agitated question, as to the extent of the Atonement, completely at rest. Posterity will thank the author till the latest ages, for his illustrious arguments." — *New York Evangelist.*

THE UNION OF THE HOLY SPIRIT AND THE CHURCH, in the Conversion of the World. By THOMAS W. JENKYN, D.D. 12mo., cloth. Price 85 cents.

"The discussion is eminently scriptural, placing its grand theme, the union of the Holy Spirit and the Church in the conversion of the world, in a very clear and affecting light." — *Christian Watchman.*

"A very excellent work upon a very important subject. The author seems to have studied it in all its bearings, as presented to his contemplation in the sacred volume." — *London Evangelical Magazine.*

"Fine talent, sound learning, and scriptural piety pervade every page. It is impossible that it can be read without producing great effects. Mr. Jenkyn deserves the thanks of the whole body of Christians for a book which will greatly benefit the world and the church." — *London Evangelist.*

ANTIOCH; Or, Increase of Moral Power in the Church of Christ. By Rev. P. CHURCH. With an Introductory Essay, by BARON STOW, D.D. 18mo., cloth. Price 50 cents.

"It is a book of close and consecutive thought, and treats of subjects which are of the deepest interest, at the present time, to the churches of this country The author is favorably known to the religious public, as an original thinker, and a forcible writer." — *Christian Reflector.*

"By some this book will be condemned, by many it will be read with pleasure, because it analyzes and renders tangible, principles that have been vaguely conceived in many minds, reluctantly promulgated, and hesitatingly believed. We advise our brethren to read the book, and judge for themselves." — *Baptist Record.*

"It is the work of an original thinker, on a subject of great practical interest to the church. It is replete with suggestions, which, in our view, are eminently worthy of consideration." — *Phila. Christian Observer.*

THE IMITATION OF CHRIST. By THOMAS A KEMPIS. With an Introductory Essay, by T. CHALMERS, D.D. A new and improved edition. Edited by H. MALCOM, D.D. 18mo., cloth. Price 38 cents.

THE PERSON AND WORK OF CHRIST. By ERNEST SARTORIUS, D. D. Translated from the German, by Rev. O. S. STEARNS, A. M. Cloth. 42 cents.

"A work of much ability, and presenting the argument in a style that will be new to most American readers, it will deservedly attract attention." — *N. Y. Observer.*

PHILOSOPHY AND PHILOLOGY.

ANCIENT LITERATURE AND ART; Or, Essays on Classical Studies, with the Biography and Correspondence of Eminent Philologists. By BARNAS SEARS, of Newton; B. B. EDWARDS, of Andover; and C. C. FELTON, of Cambridge. 12mo. Cloth. Price, $1 25.

"The object of the accomplished gentlemen who have engaged in its preparation has been, to foster and extend among educated men, in this country, the already growing interest in classical studies. The design is a noble and generous one, and has been executed with a taste and good sense that do honor both to the writers and the publishers. The book is one which deserves a place in the library of every educated man. To those now engaged in classical study it cannot fail to be highly useful, while to the more advanced scholar, it will open new sources of interest and delight in the unforgotten pursuits of his earlier days." — *Providence Journal.*

GESENIUS'S HEBREW GRAMMAR. Translated from the Eleventh German Edition. By T. J. CONANT, Prof. of Hebrew and of Biblical Criticism and Interpretation in the Theol. Institution at Hamilton, N. Y. With a Course of Exercises in Hebrew Grammar, and a Hebrew Chrestomathy, prepared by the Translator. 8vo. cloth. Price $2.00.

"*** Special reference has been had in the arrangement, illustrations, the addition of the Course of Exercises, the Chrestomathy, &c., to adapt it to the wants of those who may wish to pursue the study of Hebrew without the aid of a teacher.

LIFE OF GODFREY WILLIAM VON LIEBNITZ. On the basis of the German Work of Dr. G. E. Guhrauer. By JOHN M. MACKIE. 16mo. cloth. Price 75 cents.

"The peculiar relation which Liebnitz sustained during his life to Locke and Newton may partly account for the fact that a biography of this great man has been so long wanting in the English language. . . . We commend this book, not only to scholars and men of science, but to all our readers who love to contemplate the life and labors of a great and good man. It merits the special notice of all who are interested in the business of education, and deserves a place by the side of Brewster's Life of Newton, in all the libraries of our schools, academies, and literary institutions."— *Christian Watchman.*

"There is perhaps no case on record of a single man who has so gone the rounds of human knowledge as did Liebnitz: he was not a recluse, like Spinoza and Kant, but went from capital to capital, and associated with kings and premiers. All branches of thought were interesting to him, and he seems in pursuing all to have been actuated not by ambition, but by a sincere desire to promote the knowledge and welfare of mankind. — *Christian World.*

LIFE OF ROGER WILLIAMS, The Founder of the State of Rhode Island. By WM. GAMMELL, Prof. in Brown University. With a Likeness. 12mo. cloth. Price 75 cents.

"Mr. Gammell's fine belles-letters attainments have enabled him to present his distinguished subject in the most captivating light. So far as the work touches controversies which reach and influence the present times, it is our privilege as well as duty to read it as a private citizen, and not as a public journalist. Its mechanical execution is in the usually neat style of the respectable publishers." — *Christian Alliance.*

"This life has many virtues — brevity, simplicity, fairness. Though written by a Rhode Island man, and warm in its approval of Roger Williams, it is not unjust to his Puritan opponents, but only draws such deductions as were unavoidable from the premises. It is the life of a *good* man, and we read with grateful complacency the commendation of his excellences."

Christian World.

WORKS ON MISSIONS.

THE MISSIONARY ENTERPRISE; A Collection of Discourses on Christian Missions, by American Authors. Edited by BARON STOW, D.D. 12mo., cloth. Price 85 cents.

"If we desired to put into the hands of a foreigner a fair exhibition of the capacity and spirit of the American church, we would give him this volume. You have here thrown together a few discourses, preached from time to time, by different individuals, of different denominations, as circumstances have demanded them; and you see the stature and feel the pulse of the American Church in these discourses with a certainty not to be mistaken.

"You see the high talent of the American church. We venture the assertion, that no nation in the world has such an amount of forceful, available talent in its pulpit. The energy, directness, scope, and intellectual spirit of the American church is wonderful. In this book, the discourses by Dr. Beecher, Pres. Wayland, and the Rev. Dr. Stone of the Episcopal church, are among the very highest exhibitions of logical correctness, and burning, popular fervor. This volume will have a wide circulation."—*The New Englander.*

"This work contains fifteen sermons on Missions, by Rev. Drs. Wayland, Griffin, Anderson, Williams, Beecher, Miller, Fuller, Beman, Stone, Mason, and by Rev. Messrs. Kirk, Stow, and Ide. It is a rich treasure, which ought to be in the possession of every American Christian." — *Carolina Baptist.*

THE GREAT COMMISSION; Or, the Christian Church constituted and charged to convey the Gospel to the world. A Prize Essay. By JOHN HARRIS, D.D. With an Introductory Essay, by W. R. WILLIAMS, D.D. Sixth thousand. 12mo., cloth. Price $1.00.

"His plan is original and comprehensive. In filling it up the author has interwoven facts with rich and glowing illustrations, and with trains of thought that are sometimes almost resistless in their appeals to the conscience. The work is not more distinguished for its arguments and its genius, than for the spirit of deep and fervent piety that pervades it." — *The Dayspring.*

"Its style is remarkably chaste and elegant. Its sentiments richly and fervently evangelical, its argumentation conclusive." — *Zion's Herald, Boston.*

"To recommend this work to the friends of missions of all denominations would be but faint praise; the author deserves and will undoubtedly receive the credit of having applied a new lever to that great moral machine which, by the blessing of God, is destined to evangelize the world."
Christian Secretary, Hartford.

"We hope that the volume will be attentively and prayerfully read by the whole church, which are clothed with the "Great Commission" to evangelize the world, and that they will be moved to an immediate discharge of its high and momentous obligations.—*N. E. Puritan, Boston.*

THE KAREN APOSTLE; Or, Memoir of KO THAH-BYU, the first Karen convert with notices concerning his Nation. By the Rev. FRANCIS MASON. Edited by Prof. H. J. RIPLEY. Fifth thousand. 18mo., cloth. Price 25 cents.

"This is a work of thrilling interest, containing the history of a remarkable man, and giving, also, much information respecting the Karen Mission, heretofore unknown in this country. It gives an account, which must be attractive, from its novelty, of a people that have been but little known and visited by missionaries, till within a few years. The baptism of Ko Thah-Byu, in 1828, was the beginning of the mission, and at the end of these twelve years, twelve hundred and seventy Karens are officially reported as members of the churches, in good standing. The mission has been carried on pre-eminently by the Karens themselves, and there is no doubt, from much touching evidence contained in this volume, that they are a people peculiarly susceptible to religious impressions."

MEMOIRS OF DISTINGUISHED MISSIONARIES.

MEMOIR OF ANN H. JUDSON, late Missionary to Burmah. By Rev. James D. Knowles. With a likeness. 12mo., fine Edition, price 85 cents. 18mo. Price 58 cents.

"We are particularly gratified to perceive a new edition of the Memoirs of Mrs. Judson. She was an honor to our country — one of the most noble-spirited of her sex. It cannot, therefore, be surprising, that so many editions, and so many thousand copies of her life and adventures have been sold. The name — the long career of suffering — the self-sacrificing spirit of the retired country-girl, have spread over the whole world; and the heroism of her apostleship and almost martyrdom, stands out a living and heavenly beacon-fire, amid the dark midnight of ages, and human history and exploits. She was the first *woman* who resolved to become a missionary to heathen countries." — *American Traveller.*

"This is one of the most interesting pieces of female biography which has ever come under our notice. No quotation, which our limits allow, would do justice to the facts, and we must, therefore, refer our readers to the volume itself. It ought to be immediately added to every family library."
London Miscellany.

MEMOIR OF GEORGE DANA BOARDMAN, Late Missionary to Burmah, containing much intelligence relative to the Burman mission. By Rev. Alonzo King. Embellished with a Likeness; a beautiful Vignette, representing the baptismal scene just before his death; and a drawing of his tomb. By Rev. H. Malcom, D.D. 12mo. Price 75 cents.

"One of the brightest luminaries of Burmah is extinguished — dear brother Boardman is gone to his eternal rest. He fell gloriously at the head of his troops — in the arms of victory, — thirty-eight wild Karens having been brought into the camp of king Jesus since the beginning of the year, besides the thirty-two that were brought in during the two preceding years. Disabled by wounds, he was obliged, through the whole of the last expedition, to be carried on a litter; but his presence was a host, and the Holy Spirit accompanied his dying whispers with almighty influence." — *Rev. Dr. Judson.*

MEMOIR OF MRS. HENRIETTA SHUCK, The first American Female Missionary to China. By Rev. J. B. Jeter. With a Likeness. Fourth thousand. 18mo. Price 50 cents.

"The style of the author is sedate and perspicuous, such as we might expect from his known piety and learning, his attachment to missions, and the amiable lady whose memory he embalms. The book will be extensively read and eminently useful, and thus the ends sought by the author will be happily secured. We think we are not mistaken in this opinion. Those who are interested in China, that large opening field for the glorious conquests of divine truth, will be interested in this Memoir. To the friends of missions generally, the book is commended, as worthy of an attentive perusal." — *The Family Visitor, Boston.*

MEMOIR OF REV. WILLIAM G. CROCKER, Late Missionary in West Africa, among the Bassas, Including a History of the Mission. By R. B. Medbery. With a likeness. 18mo. Price 62½ cents.

"Our acquaintance with the excellent brother, who is the subject of this Memoir, will be long and fondly cherished. This volume, prepared by a *lady*, of true taste and talent, and of a kindred spirit, while it is but a just tribute to his worth, will, we doubt not, furnish lessons of humble and practical piety, and will give such facts relative to the mission to which he devoted his life, as to render it worthy a distinguished place among the religious and missionary biography which has so much enriched the family of God." - *Watchman.*

REV. HARVEY NEWCOMB'S WORKS.

HOW TO BE A LADY; A Book for Girls, containing useful hints on the formation of character. Fifth thousand. 18mo., gilt cloth. Price 50 cents.

"Having daughters of his own, and having been many years employed in writing for the young, he hopes to be able to offer some good advice, in an entertaining way, for girls or misses, between the ages of eight and fifteen. His object is, to assist them in forming their characters upon the best model that they may become well-bred, intelligent, refined, and good; and then they will be real *ladies*, in the highest sense." — *Preface.*

"They are full of wholesome and judicious counsels, which are well fitted to preserve the young from the numberless evils to which they are exposed, and to mould them to virtue and usefulness. There is a directness and earnestness pervading the whole, which must secure for it a ready access to the youthful mind and heart." — *Albany Argus.*

HOW TO BE A MAN; A Book for Boys, containing useful hints on the formation of character. Fifth thousand. 18mo., gilt cloth. Price 50 cents.

"My design in writing has been to contribute something towards forming the character of those who are to be our future electors, legislators, governors, judges, ministers, lawyers, and physicians, — after the best model. It is intended for boys — or, if you please, for *young* gentlemen, in early youth, from eight or ten to fifteen or sixteen years of age." — *Preface.*

"They contain wise and important counsels and cautions, adapted to the young, and made entertaining by the interesting style and illustrations of the author. They are fine mirrors, in which are reflected the prominent lineaments of the *Christian young gentleman and young lady*. The execution of the works is of the first order, and the books will afford elegant and most profitable presents for the young." — *American Pulpit.*

ANECDOTES FOR BOYS; Entertaining Anecdotes and Narratives, illustrative of principles and character. 18mo., gilt cloth. Price 42 cents.

"Nothing has a greater interest for a youthful mind than a well-told story, and no medium of conveying moral instructions so attractive or so successful. The influence of all such stories is far more powerful when the child is assured that they are true. The book before us is conducted upon these ideas. It is made up of a series of anecdotes, every one of which inculcates some excellent moral lesson. We cannot too highly approve of the book, or too strongly recommend it to parents." — *Western Continent, Baltimore.*

ANECDOTES FOR GIRLS; Entertaining Anecdotes and Narratives, illustrative of principles and character. 18mo., gilt cloth. Price 42 cents.

"There is a charm about these two beautiful volumes not to be mistaken. They are deeply interesting and instructive, without being fictitious. The anecdotes are many, short, and spirited, with a moral drawn from each, somewhat after the manner of [illegible]; and no youth can read them without finding something therein adapted to every age, condition, and duty of life. We commend it to families and schools." — *Albany Spectator.*

"He desires to instruct rather than to dazzle; to infuse correct principles into the minds and the heart of the young, than cater to a depraved appetite for romantic excitement. We cordially commend these volumes to all parents and children." — *Christian Alliance.*

CHRISTIANITY DEMONSTRATED in four distinct and independent series of proofs; with an explanation of the Types and Prophecies concerning the Messiah. 12mo. Price 75 cents.

*** The object of the writer has been to classify and condense the evidence, that the whole force of each particular kind might be seen at one view. He has also aimed to render the work *practical*, so as to have it a book to be *read* as well as *studied*. The Types and Prophecies furnish an important species of evidence, and are rich in instruction upon the way of Salvation.

THE FOUR GOSPELS, WITH NOTES. Chiefly Explanatory intended principally for Sabbath School Teachers and Bible Classes, and as an aid to Family Instruction. By H. J. RIPLEY. With a Map of Palestine. Eighth thousand. 12mo., half morocco. Price $1.25.

"The undersigned, having examined Professor Ripley's Notes on the Gospels, can recommend them with confidence to all who need such helps in the study of the sacred Scriptures. Those passages which all can understand are left 'without note or comment,' and the principal labor is devoted to the explanation of such parts as need to be explained and rescued from the perversions of errorists, both the ignorant and the learned. The practical suggestions at the close of each chapter, are not the least valuable portion of the work. Most cordially, for the sake of truth and righteousness, do we wish for these Notes a wide circulation."

BARON STOW,	R. H. NEALE,	R. TURNBULL,
DANIEL SHARP,	J. W. PARKER,	N. COLVER,
WM. HAGUE,	R. W. CUSHMAN,	J. W. BOSWORTH.

THE ACTS OF THE APOSTLES, WITH NOTES. Chiefly Explanatory. Designed for Teachers in Sabbath Schools and Bible Classes, and as an Aid to Family Instruction. By Prof. H. J. Ripley. With a Map of Paul's Travels. Third Thousand. 12mo., half morocco. Price 75 cents.

"On examining the contents, we are favorably impressed, first, by the wonderful perspicuity, simplicity, and comprehensiveness of the author's style; secondly, by the completeness and systematic arrangement of the work, in all its parts; thirdly, by the correct theology, solid instruction, and consistent explanations of difficult passages. The work cannot fail to be received with favor." — *Christian Reflector, Boston.*

CRUDEN'S CONDENSED CONCORDANCE. A Complete Concordance to the Holy Scriptures; by ALEXANDER CRUDEN, M.A. A New and Condensed Edition, with an Introduction; by Rev. DAVID KING, LL.D. Fifth Thousand. Price, in Boards, $1.25; Sheep, $1.50.

*** This edition is printed from English plates, and is a full and fair copy of all that is valuable in Cruden as a Concordance. The condensation of the quotations of Scripture, arranged under their most obvious heads, while it diminishes the bulk of the work, greatly facilitates the finding of any required passage.

"Those who have been acquainted with the various works of this kind now in use, well know that Cruden's Concordance far excels all others. Yet we have in this edition the best made better. That is, the present is better adapted to the purposes of a Concordance, by the erasure of superfluous references, the omission of unnecessary explanations, and the contraction of quotations, &c.; it is better as a manual, and is better adapted by its price to the means of many who need and ought to possess such a work, than the former larger and expensive edition." — *Boston Recorder.*

"The new, condensed, and cheap work prepared from the voluminous and costly one of Cruden, opportunely fills a chasm in our Biblical literature. The work has been examined critically, and pronounced complete and accurate." — *Baptist Record, Philadelphia.*

"This is the very work of which we have long felt the need, and we are much pleased that its enterprising publishers can now furnish the student of the Bible with a work which he so much needs at so cheap a rate."
Advent Herald, Boston.

"We cannot see but it is, in all points, as valuable a book of reference, for ministers and Bible students, as the larger edition." — *Christian Reflector.*

ELEGANT MINIATURE VOLUMES.

Gilt Edges and beautifully Ornamented Covers. Price 31¼ cents each.

DAILY MANNA for Christian Pilgrims. By Rev. B. STOW. D.D

THE ATTRACTIONS OF HEAVEN. Edited by the Rev. H. A. GRAVES.

THE YOUNG COMMUNICANT. An Aid to the Right Understanding and Spiritual Improvement of the Lord's Supper.

THE ACTIVE CHRISTIAN. By JOHN HARRIS, D.D.

THE BIBLE AND THE CLOSET: Or, how we may read the Scriptures with the most spiritual profit. And Secret Prayer successfully managed. Edited by Rev. J. O. Choules.

THE MARRIAGE RING, or how to make Home Happy. From the writings of J. A. JAMES.

LYRIC GEMS. A Collection of Original and Select Sacred Poetry. Edited by Rev. S. F. SMITH.

THE CASKET OF JEWELS, for Young Christians. By JAMES, EDWARDS, and HARRIS.

THE CYPRESS WREATH. A Book of Consolation for those who Mourn. Edited by Rev. R. W. GRISWOLD.

THE MOURNER'S CHAPLET. An Offering of Sympathy for Bereaved Friends. Edited by JOHN KEESE.

THE FAMILY CIRCLE. Its Affections and Pleasures. Edited by the Rev. H. A. GRAVES.

THE FAMILY ALTAR. Or the Duty, Benefits, and Mode of conducting Family Worship.

Sets of the above, in neat boxes, and forming a beautiful "Miniature Library" in 12 Vols. Price $3.75.

THE SILENT COMFORTER. A Companion for the Sick Room. By Mrs. LOUISA PAYSON HOPKINS.

GOLDEN GEMS; for the Christian. Selected from the writings of Rev. JOHN FLAVEL, with a Memoir of the Author, by Rev JOSEPH BANVARD.

DOUBLE MINIATURES. PRICE 50 CENTS EACH.

THE WEDDING GIFT: Or, the Duties and Pleasures of Domestic Life.
THE YOUNG CHRISTIAN'S GUIDE to the Doctrines and Duties of a Religious Life.
THE MOURNER COMFORTED.
THE CHRISTIAN'S PRIVATE COMPANION.
CONSOLATION FOR THE AFFLICTED.
THE SILENT COMFORTER. DAILY DUTIES.

THE OLD RED SANDSTONE;

OR, NEW WALKS IN AN OLD FIELD.

BY HUGH MILLER.

FROM THE FOURTH LONDON EDITION — ILLUSTRATED.

12mo, cloth, price $1,25.

A writer, in noticing Mr. Miller's "First Impressions of England and the People," in the *New Englander*, of May, 1850, commences by saying, "We presume it is not necessary formally to introduce Hugh Miller to our readers; the author of 'The Old Red Sandstone' placed himself, by that production, which was first, among the most successful geologists and the best writers of the age. We well remember with what mingled emotion and delight we first read that work. Rarely has a more remarkable book come from the press. * * For, besides the important contributions which it makes to the science of Geology, it is written in a style which places the author at once among the most accomplished writers of the age. * * He proves himself to be in prose what Burns has been in poetry. We are not extravagant in saying that there is no geologist living who, in the descriptions of the phenomena of the science, has united such accuracy of statement with so much poetic beauty of expression. We do not hesitate to place Mr. Miller in the front rank of English prose writers. His style has a classic purity and elegance, which remind one of Goldsmith and Irving, while there is an ease and a naturalness in the illustrations of the imagination, which belong only to men of true genius."

A writer in the *American Traveller*, in noticing the work, says, —

"The admirer of scenery, of all that is picturesque in nature, cannot fail to be delighted with his graphic delineations. Above all, the good citizen, the religious man, will read this highly interesting volume with no ordinary satisfaction."

"The excellent and lively work of our meritorious, self-taught countryman, Mr. Miller, is as admirable for the clearness of its descriptions, and the sweetness of its composition, as for the purity and gracefulnes which pervade it." — *Edinburgh Review.*

"This admirable work evinces talent of the highest order, a deep and healthful moral feeling, a perfect command of the finest language, and a beautiful union of philosophy and poetry. No geologist can peruse this volume without instruction and delight." — *Silliman's American Journal of Science.*

"Mr. Miller's exceedingly interesting book on this formation is just the sort of work to render any subject popular. It is written in a remarkably pleasing style, and contains a wonderful amount of information." — *Westminster Review.*

"In Mr. Miller's charming little work will be found a very graphic description of the Old Red Fishes. I know not of a more fascinating volume on any branch of British geology." — *Mantell's Medals of Creation.*

"Mr. Miller had elevated himself to a position which any man, in any sphere of life, might well envy He had seen some of his papers on geology, written in a style so beautiful and poetical as to throw plain geologists, like himself, in the shade." — *Sir Roderick Murchison.*

"A geological work, small in size, unpretending in spirit and manner; its contents, the conscientious narration of fact; its style, the beautiful simplicity of truth; and altogether possessing, for a rational reader, an interest superior to that of a novel." — *Dr. J. Pye Smith.*

THE EARTH AND MAN:

Lectures on Comparative Physical Geography, in its Relation to the History of Mankind.

By Arnold Guyot, Prof. Phys. Geo. and Hist., Neuchatel.

Translated from the French by Prof. C. C. Felton. *With Illustrations.*

12mo. Price, $1 25.

"The work is one of high merit, exhibiting a wide range of knowledge, great research, and a philosophical spirit of investigation. Its perusal will well repay the most learned in such subjects, and give new views to all of man's relation to the globe he inhabits." — *Silliman's Journal.*

"To the reader we shall owe no apology, if we have said enough to excite his curiosity, and to persuade him to look to the book itself for further instruction." — *North American Review.*

"The grand idea of the work is happily expressed by the author, where he calls it the *geographical march of history.* * * * The man of science will hail it as a beautiful generalization from the facts of observation. The Christian, who trusts in a merciful Providence, will draw courage from it, and hope yet more earnestly for the redemption of the most degraded portions of mankind. Faith, science, learning, poetry, taste, in a word, genius, have liberally contributed to the production of the work under review. Sometimes we feel as if we were studying a treatise on the exact sciences; at others, it strikes the ear like an epic poem. Now it reads like history, and now it sounds like prophecy. It will find readers in whatever language it may be published; and in the elegant English dress which it has received from the accomplished pen of the translator, it will not fail to interest, instruct, and inspire." — *Christian Examiner.*

"These lectures form one of the most valuable contributions to geographical science that has ever been published in this country. They invest the study of geography with an interest which will, we doubt not, surprise and delight many. They will open an entire new world to most readers, and will be found an invaluable aid to the teacher and student of geography." — *Evening Traveller.*

"We venture to pronounce this one of the most interesting and instructive books which have come from the American press for many a month. The science of which it treats, is comparatively of recent origin; but it is of great importance, not only on account of its connections with other branches of knowledge, but for its bearing upon many of the interests of society. It abounds with the richest interest and instruction to every intelligent reader, and is especially fitted to awaken enthusiasm and delight in all who are devoted to the study, either of natural science or the history of mankind." — *Providence Journal.*

"Geography is here presented under a new and attractive phase; it is no longer a dry description of the features of the earth's surface. The influence of soil, scenery, and climate upon character, has not yet received the consideration due to it from historians and philosophers. In the volume before us, the profound investigations of Humboldt, Ritter, and others, in Physical Geography, are presented in a popular form, and with the clearness and vivacity so characteristic of French treatises on science. The work should be introduced into our higher schools." — *The Independent, New York.*

"Geography is here made to assume a dignity not heretofore attached to it. The knowledge communicated in these lectures is curious, unexpected, absorbing." — *Christian Mirror, Portland.*

VALUABLE SCHOOL BOOKS.

ELEMENTS OF MORAL SCIENCE. By FRANCIS WAYLAND, D.D. President of Brown University, and Professor of Moral Philosophy. Thirty-sixth Thousand. 12mo., cloth. Price $1.25.

From Rev. Wilbur Fisk, President of the Wesleyan University.

"I have examined it with great satisfaction and interest. The work was greatly needed, and is well executed. Dr. Wayland deserves the grateful acknowledgments and liberal patronage of the public. I need say nothing further to express my high estimate of the work, than that we shall immediately adopt it as a text-book in our university."

From Hon. James Kent, late Chancellor of New York.

"The work has been read by me attentively and thoroughly, and I think very highly of it. The author himself is one of the most estimable of men, and I do not know of any ethical treatise, in which our duties to God and to our fellow-men are laid down with more precision, simplicity, clearness, energy, and truth."

"The work of Dr. Wayland has arisen gradually from the necessity of correcting the false principles and fallacious reasonings of Paley. It is a radical mistake, in the education of youth, to permit any book to be used by students as a text-book, which contains erroneous doctrines, especially when these are fundamental, and tend to vitiate the whole system of morals. We have been greatly pleased with the method which President Wayland has adopted; he goes back to the simplest and most fundamental principles; and, in the statement of his views, he unites perspicuity with conciseness and precision. In all the author's leading fundamental principles we entirely concur." — *Biblical Repository.*

MORAL SCIENCE ABRIDGED, by the Author, and adapted to the use of Schools and Academies. Twenty-fifth Thousand. 18mo., half cloth. Price 25 cents.

The more effectually to meet the desire expressed for a *cheap edition*, the present edition is issued at the *reduced price of 25 cents per copy*, and it is hoped thereby to extend the benefit of moral instruction to all the youth of our land. Teachers and all others engaged in the training of youth, are invited to examine this work.

"Dr. Wayland has published an abridgment of his work, for the use of schools. Of this step we can hardly speak too highly. It is more than time that the study of moral philosophy should be introduced into all our institutions of education. We are happy to see the way so auspiciously opened for such an introduction. It has been not merely abridged, but also *re-written*. We cannot but regard the labor as well bestowed." — *North American Review.*

"We speak that we do know, when we express our high estimate of Dr. Wayland's ability in teaching Moral Philosophy, whether orally or by the book. Having listened to his instructions, in this interesting department, we can attest how lofty are the principles, how exact and severe the argumentation, how appropriate and strong the illustrations which characterize his system and enforce it on the mind." — *The Christian Witness.*

"The work of which this volume is an abridgment, is well known as one of the best and most complete works on Moral Philosophy extant. The author is well known as one of the most profound scholars of the age. That the study of Moral Science, a science which teaches *goodness*, should be a branch of education, not only in our colleges, but in our schools and academies, we believe will not be denied. The abridgment of this work seems to us admirably calculated for the purpose, and we hope it will be extensively applied to the purposes for which it is intended." · *The Mercantile Journal.*

BLAKE'S FIRST BOOK IN ASTRONONY. Designed for the Use of Common Schools. By J. L. BLAKE, D.D. Illustrated by Steel Plate Engravings. 8vo., cloth back. Price 50 cents.

From E. Hinckley, Prof. of Mathematics in Maryland University.

"I am much indebted to you for a copy of the First Book in Astronomy. It is a work of utility and merit, far superior to any other which I have seen. The author has selected his topics with great judgment, — arranged them in admirable order, — exhibited them in a style and manner at once tasteful and philosophical. Nothing seems wanting, — nothing redundant. It is truly a very beautiful and attractive book, calculated to afford both pleasure and profit to all who may enjoy the advantage of perusing it."

From B. Field, Principal of the Hancock School, Boston.

"I know of no other work on Astronomy so well calculated to interest and instruct young learners in this sublime science."

From Isaac Foster, Instructor of Youth, Portland.

"I have examined Blake's First Book in Astronomy, and am much pleased with it. A very happy selection of topics is presented in a manner which cannot fail to interest the learner, while the questions will assist him materially in fixing in the memory what ought to be retained. It leaves the most intricate parts of the subject for those who are able to master them, and brings before the young pupil only what can be made intelligible and interesting to him."

"We are free to say, that it is, in our opinion, decidedly the best work we have any knowledge of, on the sublime and interesting subject of Astronomy. The engravings are executed in a superior style, and the mechanical appearance of the book is extremely prepossessing.—*Evening Gazette, Boston.*

"We do not hesitate to recommend it to the notice of the superintending committees, teachers, and pupils of our public schools. The definitions in the first part of the volume are given in brief and clear language, adapted to the understanding of beginners."—*State Herald, N. H.*

BLAKE'S NATURAL PHILOSOPHY. Being Conversations on Philosophy, with the addition of Explanatory Notes, Questions for Examination, and a Dictionary of Philosophical Terms. With twenty-eight steel Engravings. By J. L. BLAKE, D.D. 12mo., sheep. Price 67 cents.

*** Perhaps no work has contributed so much as this to excite a fondness for the study of Natural Philosophy in youthful minds. The familiar comparisons, with which it abounds, awaken interest, and rivet the attention of the pupil.

From Rev. J. Adams, President of Charleston College, S. C.

"I have been highly gratified with the perusal of your edition of Conversations on Natural Philosophy. The Questions, Notes, and Explanations of Terms, are valuable additions to the work, and make this edition superior to any other with which I am acquainted. I shall recommend it wherever I have an opportunity."

"We avail ourselves of the opportunity furnished us by the publication of a new edition of this deservedly popular work, to recommend it, not only to those instructors who may not already have adopted it, but also generally to all readers who are desirous of obtaining information on the subjects on which it treats. By Questions arranged at the bottom of the pages, in which the collateral facts are arranged, he directs the attention of the learner to the principal topics. Mr. Blake has also added many Notes, which illustrate the passages to which they are appended, and the Dictionary of Philosophical Terms is a useful addition." — *U. S. Literary Gazette.*

SEVENTH THOUSAND.

WAYLAND'S POLITICAL ECONOMY,

FOR COMMON SCHOOLS.

☞ *The success which has attended the abridgment of " The Elements of Moral Science," has induced the author to prepare an abridgment of this work. In this case, as in the other, the work has been wholly re-written, and adapted to the attainments of youth."*

From the Boston Recorder.

"The original work of the author, on Political Economy, has already been noticed in our pages; and the present abridgment stands in no need of a recommendation from us. We may be permitted, however, to say that both the rising and risen generations are deeply indebted to Dr. Wayland, for the skill and power he has put forth to bring a highly important subject distinctly before them, within such narrow limits. Though 'abridged for the use of academies,' it deserves to be introduced into every private family, and to be studied by every man who has an interest in the wealth and prosperity of his country. It is a subject little understood, even practically, by thousands, and still less understood theoretically. It is to be hoped, this will form a class-book, and be faithfully studied in our academies; and that it will find its way into every family library; not there to be shut up unread, but to afford rich material for thought and discussion in the family circle. It is fitted to enlarge the mind, to purify the judgment, to correct erroneous popular impressions, and assist every man in forming opinions of public measures, which will abide the test of time and experience."

From the New York Transcript.

"An abridgment of this clear, common-sense work, designed for the use of academies, is just published. We rejoice to see such treatises spreading among the people; and we urge all who would be intelligent freemen, to read them."

From the New York Observer.

"We can say, with safety, that the topics are well selected and arranged; that the author's name is a guarantee for more than usual excellence. We wish it an extensive circulation."

From the Daily Advocate.

"It is well adapted to high schools, and embraces the soundest system of republican political economy of any treatise extant."

From JAMES SHANNON, *President of the College of Louisiana.*

"I have rarely met with a work of the kind with which I was more pleased, than with Dr. Wayland's Elements of Political Economy, Abridged. The highest commendation I can give his larger work, and also his Elements of Moral Science is, that I have introduced them into my classes, as by far the best text-books, on those branches, that I have ever seen. The latter work, with the exception of a few chapters, I regard almost perfect."

www.ingramcontent.com/pod-product-compliance
Lightning Source LLC
LaVergne TN
LVHW020222110826

845151LV00003B/797

* 9 7 8 1 4 2 5 5 3 3 1 0 6 *